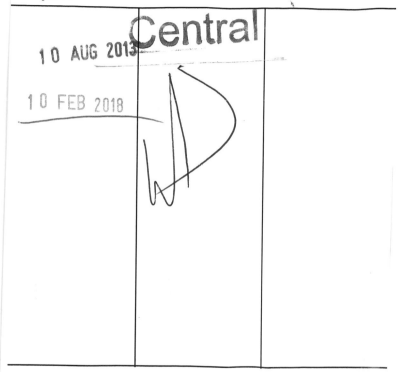

STUART BROAD
MY WORLD IN CRICKET

STUART BROAD
MY WORLD IN CRICKET

PHOTOGRAPHY BY PHILIP BROWN

SIMON &
SCHUSTER

London · New York · Sydney · Toronto · New Delhi

A CBS COMPANY

First published in Great Britain by Simon & Schuster UK Ltd, 2012
A CBS Company

1 3 5 7 9 10 8 6 4 2

Simon & Schuster UK Ltd
1st Floor
222 Gray's Inn Road
London WC1X 8HB

www.simonandschuster.co.uk

Simon & Schuster Australia,
Sydney

Simon & Schuster India,
New Delhi

A CIP catalogue record for this book is
available from the British Library

ISBN 978-1-47110-156-4

Designed by Jacqui Caulton

Printed and bound in Great Britain by
Butler Tanner and Dennis, Frome, Somerset

CONTENTS

the time, so you will find some of the most up-to-date ideas on the game within these pages.

INTRODUCTION

One of my most important philosophies is the importance of trial and error; you've got to try out something to know if it's going to work for you.

When I came up with the idea of writing this book, I knew what it was I wanted to achieve with it. I wanted to share the insight I have picked up into how to play the game. I've been learning about cricket from my earliest days messing about in the garden at home. Now, of course, I have the chance to work with the very best coaches, and to play with and against some of the world's top cricketers. I'm learning from them all the time, and I wanted to pass on some of that knowledge in this book. Cricket is changing all the time, so you will find some of the most up-to-date ideas on the game within these pages.

The target audience is quite broad, if you'll forgive the pun. If you're a 40-year-old club cricketer who has seen it all and you still enjoy playing on a Saturday afternoon, there are some useful mental techniques or training exercises in here that you can put into practice. Alternatively, if you're a 14-year-old kid who's besotted by cricket, there's plenty to learn, whether it is trying different things in the nets or coming up with new ways to play the game.

One of my most important philosophies in cricket is the importance of trial and error; in other words, you've got to try out something to know if it's going to work for you. So I hope the book will provide lots of different ideas for people to try out; some may not work, but others certainly will.

One or two chapters are quite technical, but I'm not trying to provide a definitive coaching manual here. I've always believed that it is best to go with what feels natural. I'd never be the sort of coach who would say that such a way is the only way to play a particular shot. As we've seen, some of the greatest players in the world don't necessarily do things the way they 'should'. Look at Brian Lara, he almost used to jump into his 'trigger' (the movement he makes as the bowler delivers the ball), but his method worked for him. Lasith Malinga of Sri Lanka is arguably the best twenty20 bowler in the world, but no one would try to coach someone to bowl the same way he does. He is a one-off, and his unusual bowling action comes naturally to him.

Those examples help explain why I believe it's important that everyone finds their own way of doing things, but they also need to know what things to try. I hope this book will provide some helpful suggestions. However experienced a player is, there is always an opportunity to try new things. In my professional career, I have experimented with my techniques – I went through a stage of triggering back and across to see if that would help my development as a player. Previously, as a youngster, I watched what Matthew Hayden did or what Andy Caddick did and then tried it out in the garden. I'm still learning from the guys I play alongside and against.

But having the correct techniques will take a player only so far, if he doesn't know when to apply them or why they are important – something that some guides omit to point out. All the techniques I describe in this book are related to parts of my game and I explain when I would try to utilise them on the pitch. This is the critical part of cricket: it's no good learning how to play the perfect cover drive if you don't know when to play it or why you would want to. It's pointless showing off your great hook shot, if there are two fielders stationed out in the deep waiting to catch the ball. Sometimes you have to forget your best shot and look for other options. You have to train smart and play smart.

The other aspect I believe can really help people is if they learn how to overtrain. For example, if your club has a bowling machine, try facing it at a slightly faster pace than you would normally come up against. When you try to play the same shot during a game, it won't necessarily seem any easier, but you will certainly feel as though you have more time to play it and so feel calmer when doing so.

Andrew Flintoff, Alastair Cook, Jimmy Anderson and I see the funny side during a training session – practice should be enjoyable.

I should add that this book isn't trying to teach people how to play a perfect cover drive, not least because I don't play the shot perfectly myself. A top coach would say that I probably don't bend my front knee enough or get into the ball enough. But I've taught myself how to play that shot effectively. That's all that anyone needs to achieve.

I used to struggle to hit the spinners over the top, so I went into the nets and tried to hit every ball they bowled at me back over their heads. Admittedly, it might have annoyed them a little bit, and I'd suggest it may be a shot to practise in indoor nets so that your team-mates aren't having to go and fetch the ball all the time. I don't think Graeme Swann or Monty Panesar would be too happy if I was just carting everything they bowled at me into the middle distance!

What I noticed was that the more I did it, the more I learned which balls I could hit cleanly, and which ones I couldn't and should therefore leave alone. So now, after all that practice, this has become one of the first shots I go for. If there's someone out on the boundary, I know I can chip it over the bowler's head for an easy single. I know instinctively if it's there to hit, and if it's not I will block it. There's just a moment to decide which option to take, but that decision now comes naturally, and that is thanks to overtraining.

But this book is about so much more than techniques and when to apply them, it will take the reader into many areas of my life, from the challenges involved with going on tour, to the pressures that come from being in the media eye. It will provide an insight into my world and that of a modern-day England player, revealing the fun and the hard work involved.

We will look at how a team can best work together and support each other. Above all, I wanted to share my enthusiasm for the game that so richly rewards me and to pass that on. Every day I go in to work, I have the chance to improve myself. This book is filled with many examples of little things I have learned along the way. I feel sure that they can help others too. So, enjoy the book, think about the ideas in here, and go and try them out.

The book will provide an insight into my world and that of a modern-day England player, revealing the fun and the hard work involved.

The real value of good planning comes when everyone knows before they take the field what is expected of them.

Chapter I

PLANNING

Whatever level of cricket you play, planning ahead can make a huge difference in the eventual outcome.

or the England team, planning can mean anything from long-term discussions to work out how we will try to handle certain situations we expect to face in the future, to a conversation on the pitch between Jimmy Anderson and myself about what ball we should bowl next. However, the real value of good planning comes when everyone knows before they take the field what is expected of them and what they are trying to achieve. When you know your role, there is a much better chance of a positive outcome.

LONG-TERM PLANNING

The first time I remember the England squad developing some long-term plans that really helped us out in a significant way came in the run-up to the 2009 Ashes. It began with Andy Flower looking at our recent record in the first Tests of a series. He discovered that we had often struggled to win that game, and so had to spend the rest of the series trying to catch up. Once we had identified this pattern, we could start to see how we might counteract it. Unfortunately, this doesn't mean we have entirely eliminated the problem, as The Oval Test against South Africa this summer showed.

We had already noted how frequently the first Test in a series was played at Lord's, and how often the home of cricket seemed to inspire our opponents more than it did us, giving them an extra level of energy. Perhaps this was because we have become so used to playing there now, whereas our opponents might get one or two chances in their career to play there.

A perfect example of this inspirational effect had come in the previous Ashes series in 2005, when England had started well to bowl out Australia for just 190, only to find Glenn McGrath at his best in England's reply, as he took nine wickets in the match to help his side to victory. Amazingly, England had not won an Ashes Test there since 1934. We realised we had to change this

Jimmy Anderson and I will often work together both before games and during them to develop plans against opposition batsmen.

If you prepare for it beforehand, when the time comes you've got the solution readily to hand.

pattern, and so it was decided that the venue for the first Test should not be Lord's, but Cardiff – an unfamiliar venue for the Australians.

However, the biggest element of long-term planning is usually carried out when we are looking forward to going away on tour. For example, in the summer before we went out to Australia for the Ashes series in 2010-11, we started to have conversations about how we wanted to do things when we got out there. At that early stage, we weren't talking about cricket-specific things, such as how we might dismiss certain batsmen or put other bowlers under pressure. All that could wait, because we had the games in the summer to play, and we needed to focus on our tactics for those matches, rather than distracting ourselves by worrying about the Australians.

However, we did start thinking about a series of 'what ifs'. For example, we asked ourselves how we would deal with the crowd, or any abuse they might hurl in our direction. We looked into questions about how we would handle the Australian media. And we discussed how we would deal with the wives and families coming out to join us during the tour, and what the ground-rules would be when they arrived.

It may seem to be basic stuff, but sometimes these things can become an issue, so if you prepare for it beforehand, when the time comes you've got the solution readily to hand. These conversations provided some interesting answers. For example, we came up with a way to minimise the effect that crowd abuse could have on our bowlers. Normally, after a fast bowler has completed his over, he would wander down to fine-leg between overs. The danger in doing this, however, is that the bowler could be standing close to the crowd and so become a sitting target for a whole barrage of abuse. This might upset him, or cause him to lose his focus, and so weaken our attack. Therefore, to counteract any possible danger of this happening, we decided to send Jonathan Trott down to fine-leg instead. Any abuse he received would have no impact on the bowlers and ensure that they maintained their concentration.

Another question we discussed was how we would respond to the usual Aussie talk about how they were going to beat us 5-0, or how they were going to target Andrew Strauss, or any one of the other usual lines that you expect to hear from former players or the hostile Australian media. We planned how we would respond to those sorts of comments. So, when these things were inevitably said, they didn't affect us because we'd already worked out our responses.

I recognise how fortunate we are nowadays to have the opportunity to indulge in this sort of planning, as it would not have been as possible in earlier generations. Now, however, with having an England squad and central contracts, we can carry out this sort of long-term preparation. In the old days, this would have been much harder, because there would have been far less certainty about who was actually going.

MEDIUM-TERM PLANNING

The Ashes series of 2009 was a time when I really began to learn the true value of good planning and how it could affect the eventual outcome of games. That series remains one that lingers in my mind as a truly special period in my life – though it was anything but a straightforward path to get there.

As I've already mentioned, our long-term preparation had persuaded the ECB to change the venue of the first Test to Cardiff. It didn't, of course, guarantee that we would play well, but at least it was a venue that was unable to inspire our opponents with happy memories of famous Test victories there – they'd never played there before; but then again, neither had we. We still started slowly in the series and we were lucky to escape with a draw, thanks to a determined last-wicket stand between Jimmy Anderson and Monty Panesar.

Next came the Lord's Test, when we ended up celebrating an Ashes victory there for the first time in 75 years. It was a very emotional time; I remember there were tears flowing in the changing room after we'd bowled them out to win by 115 runs. Officials from the MCC came in and presented us all with special ties to mark the occasion. Freddie Flintoff took five wickets in the second innings, which meant that he joined Gubby Allen and Ian Botham as the only men ever to get on both Lord's honours boards, for taking five wickets and scoring a century there. So that was a special personal achievement by him. At the time, I remember hoping that one day I might get a chance to join that select group. Little did I know . . .

The following summer I made 169 against Pakistan on the ground, and in May 2012 I took seven for 72 there against the West Indies. Both my career-best performances have happened at Lord's, and it is a venue that does always inspire me because of its place in cricket history. It is hard to explain why both my best performances have come there, but maybe it is because it is a pitch that can offer something to the batsman or the bowler: if the cloud comes over, the ball will often do plenty, but if the sun is shining, the track can turn into a batsman's paradise. In fact, all three of my highest Test scores have come at Lord's.

So if I was thinking of my favourite grounds, Lord's would be right up there, along with Trent Bridge, as the ones I most look forward to playing at in England. Overseas, there are two that stand out for me. Newlands in Cape Town is one. As a teenager, I spent some time in that city, and would often go past the stadium, and each time I did I would wonder what it would be like to play there, especially as it is undoubtedly one of the most picturesque settings, with Table Mountain in the background, of any in the world. When I got my chance, it was that famous occasion in 2009-10 when we had to bat out one and a half days to save the game, and the support we got then was superb. The other ground that brings me happy memories is the Kensington Oval, where I scored the winning runs in a World Cup tie early in my career, and we returned there in May 2010 to take the twenty20 World Cup.

I've often been asked whether I tense up when I am approaching a major landmark, whether it is scoring a century or taking five wickets, and I have to be honest and say 'no'. I try not to be distracted by the possibility of getting on the honours board, because the most important things are to concentrate on the job I am doing for my team, and to keep my focus on the process I go through every ball, whether I'm bowling or batting. If I start to strive that little bit more to take a fifth wicket, there is every chance I will stop doing what it is that has helped me to take four wickets. Staying as relaxed as possible is the key to getting to a landmark. Watching someone like Jonathan Trott in action is interesting here, as he is always setting himself the next small target to reach, and so does not worry about the bigger personal target.

In truth, I am much more nervous when a team-mate is approaching his century.

In truth, I am much more nervous when I'm in the changing room and a team-mate is approaching his century, or if I'm in the field and one of the other bowlers has four wickets I am concerned lest I drop a catch.

The third Test of that 2009 Ashes series, at Edgbaston, was affected by the rain, which cost almost two days' play in total, so inevitably ended up as a draw. That meant we needed to win one of the last two Tests to reclaim the Ashes, or to avoid defeat in both of them. But for some, the question was increasingly becoming not could England do it, but should I still be in the side. I had started to come under increasing media pressure over my place, because I'd taken only six wickets at an average of almost 60 thus far in the series. Admittedly, the stats weren't great. Happily, I got the backing of the coach and the selectors, who told me that I was very much a part of the team. It was just what I needed to hear. Their support meant that I went away from Birmingham feeling that I had to repay their faith in me.

I felt I had already learned a lot during that series on the pitch, but I was also developing off it as well. In particular, I discovered how to keep away from the pressure-cooker atmosphere of a big series. I already knew not to read any newspapers at all during the game. In fact, within the England team, we keep them out of the changing room and out of our hotel during the match, so that we don't get distracted by what anyone is writing about us.

But however much you try to avoid hearing what the media are saying, someone is sure to tell you – it's impossible to shut it out completely. If you're having a poor run, you can walk into a Starbuck's and a customer or

the guy behind the bar will inform you that one of the TV commentators has said your front arm isn't working well enough, or they will come up with some piece of advice. I've got a 94-year-old granddad who will regularly update me on what Bob Willis has to say about my bowling and how I can

However much you try to avoid hearing what the media are saying, someone is sure to tell you.

improve! It's all well-meaning, of course – I know they want me and the team to be successful – but hearing these things doesn't necessarily help matters, and it can begin to feel as if there is no escape. We're all good enough to know if we aren't getting the results we should be, so frequent reminders often serve simply to increase the pressure we are feeling.

In these circumstances, when things are beginning to pile in on you, that's where you have to be clever. So I went up to Loch Lomond with my dad for three days in between the Test matches, just to get away from it all. We played a bit of golf and switched off from everything to do with cricket. Because he'd experienced it for himself, he had an idea what I was going through at the time, and knew this was the best way to help me. It burst the Ashes bubble, so when I came back I felt much more fresh and relaxed – I realised there was life beyond the Tests. The result of my break was that I had much greater success when I came back.

So sometimes the best planning can simply be to plan to get away and have a break to clear your mind. Of course, if I'd have had a technical problem with my bowling at the time, I could have worked on it in the nets, but I didn't feel that was the issue. I was confident that I was bowling well enough, but I just wasn't getting the rewards, so having a little break made sense. You have to expect that your luck will eventually change if you keep doing the right things.

While my time away may have restored my spirits, the fourth Test at Headingley was a disaster for the team. We were skittled out for 102, and then Australia batted very aggressively against us and raced to a total of 445. But on a personal note, I began to see things working out for me with the ball, as I picked up six for 91 – my best Test figures at the time. That was little compensation, however, as we now knew we needed a victory in the final Test, at The Oval, if we were to win back the Ashes.

After all the planning, success at The Oval as my appeal is upheld.

We were all very focused on what we had to do, and if I was to pick out one Test match to illustrate how important good planning can be to gaining excellent results, then this match would be the one I would highlight. Our plans for how we will try to play a particular Test are decided when we have

Our plans for how we will try to play a particular Test are decided when we have a team meeting.

a team meeting four days before the game. It's important not to get ahead of yourself. With a series like the Ashes, the media build it up so much that it is vital you concentrate on seeing it simply as a game of cricket and that you don't get caught up in the hype. The old cliché of taking it one game at a time should always apply.

These pre-Test meetings are often quite detailed: we'll spend 90 minutes or two hours looking at what we want to be doing with each of our opponents and discussing our plans for them. The bowling unit will use material from the analysts, the bowling coach and our own observations to put together plans for each of the batsmen. These plans will evolve during the rubber, according to the state of the series, the form of the batsman and the type of pitch we are expecting to bowl on.

In that final Test, England batted first and made 332, a score that was below what many had expected us to make on The Oval pitch, and where most of us got in but failed to make a big score. After a light shower around lunch on the second day, Australia came out on 61 without loss in reply, looking as though they might go on to take control of the game. It was then that I got my chance.

We'd talked beforehand about the weaknesses we believed each of the Australian batsmen had, and planned our strategies around them. This was one of those times where everything went right – and I was the lucky one with the ball in my hand. Our analysts look into our opponents' statistics, to see if anyone has a high proportion of a certain type of dismissal in their career. For example, if someone has often been out LBW, then he is likely to be vulnerable to the ball nipping back at him. Sometimes we'll notice that someone is susceptible to a change of pace, and so we'll vary our pace more often.

(*Top*) Shane Watson is given out LBW, while (*below*) I celebrate another wicket as the Ashes come a step nearer.

We also look at the type of batsman we are bowling at: is he someone who goes at the ball early on, or is he instead someone who likes to leave it? If he is the latter sort of player, then by bowling straight at him, it is possible to force him into indecision, so he doesn't know whether to play it or leave it. Once the batsman has a doubt in his mind, then the bowler's chance of success is much greater, as he might play at one he would normally leave, or leave one he should defend.

In the same way that we assess how batsmen get out, we also look at their scoring wagon wheel. If, for example, a player is good at driving the ball, then having a man at short extra-cover can make him think twice about playing his favourite shot and, once more, he feels less certain about what he is doing. It is surprising how often the batsman will end up chipping one straight into the fielder's hands, as he's unable to resist playing the shot he usually relies upon.

Walking off after taking five for 37 to help set up England's crucial victory over Australia.

> **Looking back at that spell, everything went to plan – it doesn't always go like that so when it does it is very pleasing.**

I was able to use all background information during this spell and put it into practice. As a result, I ended up taking five wickets in a short time.

Meanwhile, while I was picking up these five wickets, at the other end Graeme Swann had taken the wickets of Simon Katich and Marcus North. Australia had lost seven wickets for 38 runs, and suddenly we were in charge of the Test.

Looking back at that spell (I finished with figures of five for 37), everything went to plan – it doesn't always go like that, of course, so when it does it is very pleasing. It was particularly satisfying for the analysts, who'd helped us devise those plans. That spell also earned me the Man of the Match award, and I felt I had repaid the selectors who had stood by me earlier in the summer.

From then on, we were not to be denied. Trott scored a century on his Test debut, and we declared late on day three with a lead of 545 runs. The Australians started well, getting past 200 with only two wickets down, but two run-outs in quick succession changed the mood and we were soon celebrating a victory in the match and the series.

SHORT-TERM PLANNING

Planning ahead is all well and good, but you have to learn how to adapt to what is actually happening in the match. It's a rare occasion where all your plans work out perfectly, so you also need to think carefully about what you are doing in the short term.

If I'm planning to construct an over, I obviously have to adapt according to who I'm up against. If I'm bowling at someone such as Rahul Dravid, I know that he won't get bored of leaving the ball, so if I bowl a fifth-stump line at him, I'll just be tiring myself out, because he is content to leave it all day. So with him, I try to bowl every ball at off stump, forcing him to play every delivery. Then, I might push one a little wider and, because I've got him into the habit of playing at everything, he might just go for a slightly wider one that he would normally have left and that gives me a better chance of getting a nick.

On the other hand, if I'm up against someone who is strong off his legs and likes to hit the ball straight down the ground, I would aim to drag him a little bit wider. If I bowl

Planning ahead is all well and good, but you have to learn how to adapt to what is actually happening in the match.

straight to him, I know that he's extremely likely to hit me. However, if I bowl slightly wide at him, on that fifth-stump line, I can tell that he wants to hit the ball but knows it makes sense to leave it. By making him leave the ball time after time, I can build pressure on him and perhaps eventually induce him to make a rash shot.

Typically, a lot of subcontinental players are very strong playing off their legs. Because of this, I try to bowl wider at them and drag them across their stumps, so they can still try to play in their favoured area. Then, if I fire one in at their toes, they may already be committed to coming across and I might catch them LBW or bowl them if they've not quite got their balance right.

You shouldn't just think in terms of building a plan for an over, either. For example, I might start a spell thinking I'm going to bowl away swingers for three overs, and then in the fourth ball of the fourth over show the batsman the inswinger. Sometimes you have to wait that long.

With good players, if you keep changing the type of delivery you bowl, they'll get used to it and start seeing what you're doing – noticing how you hold the ball for the different deliveries, and so on. Once they can read what you're doing, it is very difficult to catch them out. The variation needs to come as a surprise. It is the shock of something different that gets someone out. And you've got to be patient. So if you're deliberately bowling a bit wide of the stumps, what you're trying to do is to drag them across and encourage their head to go over. But you can't expect to catch them by surprise after four balls of a strategy like this – you have to build up to it.

There's one particular delivery where I've learned that surprise is a vital element, and that's bowling a bouncer. It's easy to get lured into bowling them early on in someone's innings. You might just have taken a wicket and so be feeling pumped up. But if you show a good batsman a bouncer too soon, they might get used to your pace and bounce of it. Instead, I might plan to bowl two overs constantly attacking the top of off stump, encouraging the batsman to think that they've got to get everything across to protect this area. So when

I do bowl the bouncer, it might take them by surprise and they're not in the right position to play it, which might just get me a wicket.

The third element to executing a plan is good communication between the bowlers, and this has been an integral part of England's success over the last few years. You'll notice that Jimmy Anderson and I will often field next to

It is often better to keep the bouncer as a surprise weapon.

HAT-TRICKS

For a bowler, the moment you have the most intense focus on your plan is when you have one ball to complete a hat-trick, while for a batsman the situation where you have the least time to develop a plan is when you face a hat-trick ball. I'm not sure if I am unique in this in Test cricket, but I have had the experience of taking a hat-trick and of being the hat-trick victim. Those moments were very different – and not just for the obvious reasons.

I experienced both within a few months of each other. The first one came in the first Ashes Test in Brisbane in 2010-11. It was shortly after tea on the first day, and England had started Peter Siddle's over at 197 for four, with Alastair Cook and Ian Bell going well and Australia seemingly searching for inspiration. They were just about to get it.

First Cook edged one that was angled across him to Shane Watson. The next ball was a quicker one and bowled Matt Prior, so it was my turn. I'll be honest, I had been rushed, because I still didn't have my pads on when Matty was out, so when I got out there for my first taste of Ashes cricket in Australia, I tried to take my time to gather myself and do all the usual things I do before I take strike.

But as Siddle was running in, the noise from the fans was huge. I felt like the whole ground was shaking as he charged in, with the crowd shouting 'Kill! Kill! Kill!' I remember thinking: Jesus, that's loud!

And then I was out. It wasn't that I'd done my process wrong, but something else came into my mind, and that may have led to me missing the inswinging yorker he bowled to me. To be honest, it was a good ball, and it might have got me out on plenty of other occasions. But since then, in similarly pressurised moments, I've looked to focus on shutting out everything that might distract me. On that day, my emotions took over from my gameplan, which was to concentrate on playing straight.

Some might try to console me by saying that at least I've been a part of history in this way (Siddle was only the fourth Australian bowler to take

My first ball Down Under in an Ashes Test, and I'm out LBW to hat-trick man Peter Siddle.

an Ashes hat-trick), but when you're trying to make an impact in Australia, getting out first ball isn't the way I'd want to do it!

It was quite a contrast eight months later when I had the chance to deliver my hat-trick ball. It was the second Test against India and I couldn't have chosen a better time to do it: it was a Saturday afternoon at my home ground of Trent Bridge, it was about five o'clock, so everyone had had a few beers, and the atmosphere was massive. It had been quite a sedate day up until that point, but we had taken the new ball a few overs earlier, and that gave us some added momentum. Despite that, I was so in the zone, I didn't even notice the crowd when I began my run-up. I was calm and knew what I wanted to do; it was completely the opposite of when I had faced the hat-trick ball, because then I hadn't had a chance to get in the zone.

(*Right*) Nothing could beat taking a hat-trick in front of my home crowd.

(*Below*) Praveen Kumar looks back to see the bails flying as he becomes my hat-trick victim at Trent Bridge, 2011.

First up, it had been M.S.Dhoni, who was slightly heavy-footed when he flashed at an outswinger and edged the ball to Jimmy at second slip. Then came Harbhajan Singh, who was given out LBW. Next in was Praveen Kumar.

Although I had tried to shut out the noise, I do remember that when I got back to my mark to bowl the final ball, I could feel a vibration in the ground because everyone was clapping. As I ran in, I was just trying to focus on hitting the top of off stump. But then, when I watched it back on TV, I saw how people were going wild and I saw what my hat-trick meant to people. Everyone was going up, and I simply wasn't aware of it at all at the time. But you have to work that way, as there's enough pressure for anyone trying to bowl a hat-trick ball at any level of the game, let alone in a Test match, so you've got to switch on to what you're doing and have solid and strong routines you can rely on.

It's the simplest plan of all: do the basics right. As it was, I got it just as I wanted. The ball nipped back a little off the seam and crashed into Kumar's stumps and I'd got my Test hat-trick. I held up the ball to the crowd and could finally take in their applause and revel in the moment. The plan had worked.

I believe that success in cricket comes from finding your own way to doing what works for you.

Chapter 2

TECHNICAL

A lot of my real cricket learning came in the garden, stupid as it may sound. I played non-stop at home.

In writing this book, and advising people on how to bat, I recognise that some may say that a number eight batsman is not necessarily the ideal person to learn from. Others will look at how I play my shots and spot some flaws in my technique.

Of course, they are right that I am not the best batsman in the world, and nor is my technique perfect. But for me, that criticism is missing the point. I believe that success in cricket comes from finding your own way to doing what works for you, rather than focusing simply on what the coaching manuals say is the right way to play, and then following their instructions to the letter.

To illustrate the point that there is no universally 'correct' way to play a delivery, I would give you the following example. Because I am much taller than Ian Bell or Andrew Strauss, and therefore have a greater reach than them, I might play a different shot than they would to the same ball, and yet the choices we all make would be the right ones for us, because we were all playing to our own strengths.

So when we get to the technical part of this chapter, my focus isn't going to be on showing the precise position of my feet or hands, but on when and why I play certain shots in my repertoire. From that, I hope that you will be able to pick up the relevant tips that can help you improve your own game. And, for me, that road to learning how to develop my game began in my back garden when I was just a little kid.

EARLY DAYS

For anyone interested in playing cricket, the early years are a vital period in developing your talent. As a boy, I was fortunate to go to a school where I was able to learn from good coaches, and from having the space in our garden to spend long summer days practising there. The fact that my father was a Test cricketer helped, too!

A lot of my real cricket learning came in the garden, stupid as it may sound. I played non-stop at home. Sometimes, I'd just be playing swingball, pretending to be Matthew Hayden, with windows as imaginary fielders to be avoided when I hit the ball. I learned a huge amount playing various games at home, as I was able to try out all sorts of things – even legspin – without it really mattering, as it would in the heat of a match, which is the worst time to experiment.

Until I was 14 or 15 years old, I still worked hard on my game in the garden. I would throw a tennis ball at the shed wall for hours on end and see how I could hit the rebound. Eventually, my mum had to knock the shed down, because there was a huge crack in the wall where I'd been hitting the ball! These days it's rare that people are able to spend so long practising, with so many other distractions, but I didn't see it that way. To me, it was just play, but by doing so much of it I learned such a lot.

An early appearance at Trent Bridge, aged four.

I learned a lot of my cricket in the garden as a boy. Here Gemma provides technical analysis as the wicket-keeper.

I was lucky enough to go to Oakham School in Leicestershire when I reached the age of 13, and I couldn't have had two better people to help me develop my game than Frank Hayes and David Steele, who were the coaches there. Hayes was a top-order batsman who had played for Lancashire between 1970 and 1984, and won nine England caps in the mid-1970s, making a century on his debut against the West Indies in 1973. Unfortunately for him, all his England caps would come against the men from the Caribbean, who were just beginning their long period of dominance at that time.

Steele was another top-order batsman, who had an even longer county career, and played with Hayes in the 1976 series against the West Indies. He had made his Test debut the previous summer at the age of 33, when he had taken on Dennis Lillee and Jeff Thomson at their fiery peak – in days when helmets were unheard of. His fearless approach to taking on those two earned him the admiration of cricket fans everywhere, and his heroics saw him become the BBC Sports Personality of the Year in 1975.

When I look back at what I picked up from them, however, I realise that technically they didn't do a great deal for me. What they did do, however, was even more important: they fuelled my love for the game – they were both great storytellers, and hearing their tales made me even more convinced that I wanted to become a cricketer. I remember Hayes recounting how he hit his first ball in first-class cricket straight back over the bowler's head for six.

Hayes showed me the possibilities the game could offer and the fun to be had from a cricket career.

He was inspirational in the sense that he showed me the possibilities the game could offer and the fun to be had from a cricket career.

Meanwhile, Steele was someone who grew the love of cricket in everyone who played under him. He talked about the Aussies and the tough cricket he played and how he loved the battle. His passion made us all want to turn up to practise and play. I'm sure that their methods were better for mc as a teenager than having someone telling me precisely where my front foot should be when I played an off-drive.

If I have to pinpoint a time when I developed my real love for the game, I would go for that time under their coaching – rather than what I picked up from my father or from playing in the garden. Of course, Hayes and Steele were strong characters, so if you did something wrong they'd let you know about it, but they also made sure we knew that we were there to play cricket *and* have a good time.

I began to establish myself in the school first team in 2002 (I was 16 during the summer term), and then in the following two seasons we did not lose a game as we had a very strong team. During that time Matt Boyce (now at Leicestershire) was there, Paul Cook has gone on to captain Lincolnshire, while leg-spinner Barghav Modha once took ten wickets in a game against Worksop College – pretty much unheard of at schoolboy level – so I was just left holding up an end while he got all the glory!

It may surprise some to learn that in those days I was seen as more of a batsman than a bowler, and I used to open the batting for my school side. At first, I had to rely on my technique with my batting, because that was what was going to get me through, as I wasn't big enough or strong enough to power the ball to the boundary. I'd always expected that I'd end up being tall, as my father is 6ft 4in and my uncle is something like 6ft 10in. However, it wasn't until my final year at school that I really began to grow – I put on almost a foot in a year to reach my current height of 6ft 6in. Once I had the power to go with my size, I was able to find the boundaries much more easily, but I had already developed the bedrock of a sound technique to work from.

This was the time I also began to change from being a relatively gentle medium-pace bowler to a fast bowler. Again, because I was quite small, I had relied on good control and away-swing, rather than pace and bounce, to get my wickets. But after my growth spurt, everything began to click into place: I could add some proper pace to those attributes I already had. That combination ensured that I made my debut for Leicestershire second XI in the summer of 2004 while still at school.

I was also developing my game at adult level, having started to play for Egerton Park in Melton Mowbray a few years earlier. Fortunately, the club had an exchange programme with a Melbourne team called Hopper's Crossing. The winter after I left school in 2004, I flew out to Australia to play for them. The trip came at just the right time for me. They're not one of the bigger clubs in the city, but that was no bad thing. Had I been playing First Grade cricket there, I'd most likely have been in the same team as many of the Victoria side, and maybe I would have been more of a bit-part player. That wasn't the case at Hopper's Crossing.

I went from playing school and weekend club cricket to playing tough district cricket against highly competitive Australian blokes, and suddenly I had to front up. There weren't any ECB restrictions on being able to bowl

only five overs at a time – I'd sometimes have to bowl 25 overs in a day. Because they were quite a small club, I was able to open the batting and the bowling. I was the guy they threw the ball to when they needed something to happen. They gave me responsibility, and that was crucial for my confidence at the age of 18.

Going out to Australia after my dad had had such a big impact against them in the 1986-87 tour – he scored centuries in three successive Tests to help England retain the Ashes – meant it was quite a lively atmosphere whenever the opposition learned who my father was. I had one or two extremely tough games where I'd get a couple of 30-year-old Aussie blokes who would be right in my face with some serious verbal abuse. Fortunately, I thrived off it. I've always found that when people come hard at me, I've played at my best.

But that experience in Australia also taught me one of my biggest principles: I'll never forget how this one guy had been sledging me all day, and yet at the end of the game he walked into our changing room with a

beer and said: 'Great fight today – well done.' It taught me that however tough the battle out on the field, when you get off it you're mates together. I think that typical Australian approach is a great philosophy to have: cricket may be a fierce contest on the pitch – whoever you're playing for, whether it's your club or your country – but when you walk off the field you have to be aware that it is just sport, and nothing more serious than that.

When I came back to Leicestershire for the 2005 season, after two or three second-team games, I was playing first-team cricket, making my first-class debut against Durham UCCE at the end of April and my County Championship debut a few weeks later (against Somerset).

That first season, I did quite well with my bowling, taking 30 wickets at an average of under 28, but my batting was not so successful – I averaged just 10.70, with a top score of 31. It took me a whole year to question why I was throwing away my wicket just because I was batting lower in the order than I used to at school or for my club. Even if I was coming in at ten, I began to realise that I should be making sure that I stayed there and aimed to be not out at the end. It didn't matter if I got seven or 20 not out, the important thing was still to be in the middle. Just because I was a lower-order batsman didn't mean I couldn't play myself in. Once I'd done that, I knew that if the ball was there to be hit, then I could hit it without taking too much of a risk.

So I became more switched on to my batting, and made a couple of fifties in 2006. That season I averaged over 21 – twice as high as in my debut campaign. I was beginning to work out how to play a game that suited my attributes as a batsman. It was in this period that I began to think much more deeply about how to bat. Working with some of the senior players and the coaches, I began to understand that it was in my hands to improve myself. The lessons I was learning were not so much about how to play shots, but when to play them. I realised that this is the key to it all, and what follows is there to illustrate not only how I play the various shots, but *when* I look to play them and the reasons *why* I pick one shot over another.

> # However tough the battle out on the field, when you get off it you're mates together.

PLAYING THE SHOTS

In this section, I'll explain how I try to build an innings, and what I do to ensure I'm playing the right shots at the right time. I'll assume that I am coming in to face quicker bowlers to start with (we can look at methods of dealing with spinners in a later chapter).

SCORING ONE IN THE RING

Every batsman likes to get off the mark as quickly as he can. I've found that one of the best ways to do this is to come out to bat with the mentality of 4-3-2-1-dot. It was a lesson I picked up from Michael Vaughan, who told me that he used this approach when he had that amazing Ashes series in 2002-03. During that campaign, he was in such good touch that he was pulling length balls to the boundary, and he attributed much of his success to having the right positive mental attitude.

He explained his thinking like this: if you face every ball believing that you can score a four off it, then if it is in the right place you're already primed to hit it to the boundary. But if it's not quite there, you can still push it firmly into the outfield for three or possibly two, or else you can just knock it for one instead. If the ball isn't right to hit, you can leave it or defend it. But the first instinct from the first ball should be to go in

Head over the ball, full face of the bat, this push into the covers is an easy option to rotate the strike.

to bat looking to score runs. In the England set-up, our batting coach Graham Gooch doesn't talk about us being batsmen but describes us as 'run-getters'. That's the mentality he wants to create: batsmen are there to score runs. It's a positive attitude I relish.

However, when I talk about looking to score runs straight away, I don't mean that you should be taking a big backlift and winding yourself up to heave it to all corners of the ground. It's simply about looking for the runs from the off, getting yourself into the ball, looking for four.

Of course, in most cases it's not possible to get off the mark with a boundary, but because you have set your mind to score runs, you can take the opportunity to push a single instead. In this shot, you can see I'm just easing it into the covers for one. Admittedly, there's usually gaps in the covers when I come in, as I'll often have three slips and a gully behind me, so this is an easy way for me to rotate the strike and give the established batsman the chance to face the bowling while I get used to being in the middle. But this shot can be played by anyone at any level of the game early in their innings without taking a big risk.

PUSH TO MID-ON

When I first come to the crease, I know how important it is to think about playing straight and hitting straight; playing with a cross bat early on in an innings is a high-risk strategy when you are not used to the pace and bounce of

The push to mid-on: note how balanced I am for this shot, and how my front foot is pointing in the direction of where I'm hitting the ball.

the wicket. So if I receive a delivery on the stumps, I look to hit it straight back down the pitch. You don't want to go too straight, because if you do the bowler can stop the ball, so I try to aim slightly towards mid-on as here.

There's a good reason for targeting this area, as often at mid-on in first-class cricket you will have a fast bowler fielding there. He may have bowled a lot of overs, so he may be a little bit tired (in club cricket, this is often a position where weaker or older fielders will be stationed, too). Because of this, you can nick a single and rotate the strike when you've just come in.

There's another advantage in aiming to hit straight, because if it swings back in to you, you don't fall over trying to hit it square. Every batsman loves to get off nought, and pushing the ball for one to mid-on is often the best way to do it. When you see Kevin Pietersen come in, he'll just go 'bang' and set off for a run in that area. What's more, because mid-on can't come in too tight on the single, as he has to stop the ball that has been hit hard, it is usually a safe run.

From practice and experience, you will get to know how well it's come off the bat and whether you can run – don't go if you've drilled the ball straight at him. Also bear in mind the pitch conditions when you're thinking about taking a run. For example, at Lord's the square is so fast that the ball runs quickly there, but in Australia, where the ground might also be used for football, it will usually run more slowly.

The key point with both these shots is that when I come to the crease I aim to hit everything as straight as possible so I can react to any lateral movement of the ball – even to the spinners. Of course, if there are gaps, you can look elsewhere for runs (sometimes a spinner won't have anyone on the 45, so you can sweep for a single). But in normal circumstances this is how I would look to start an innings: with either a push into the covers or to mid-on.

LEAVING THE BALL

While I always try to bat with positive intent and look to develop early momentum in my innings, believe it or not I can show these things with a strong leave. As a bowler, I know that if I bowl just outside off stump and someone has a big flash at it, it gives me a lot of encouragement. The last thing I want to be doing as a batsman is giving the bowler any encouragement when I first come to the crease.

Therefore, part of my gameplan until I get to a score of 20 is that I'll look to leave anything outside the line of my left eye when I'm in my stance (it would be outside the right eye for a right-hander) – unless it's a rank half-volley. Of course, you have to be aware that if someone is swinging it back in at you in a big way, it can trouble you. But if that is not the case, then you ought to be safe to leave it.

When I initially came into first-class cricket, I didn't have the right tempo to my batting, as I hadn't learned to leave the ball. Coming in at nine or ten, I'd often go for the shot and would find the edge. Yet once you've got to 20 and got a sweat going, it's amazing how often you can go for the same shot and it goes for four instead. This was why my batting average started off so poorly, because I was trying ambitious shots at balls I should have been leaving.

Early on in an innings, a strong leave can be a surprisingly positive move.

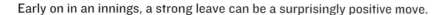

Training yourself not to go after the ball early on is not easy. The way I learned was to spend an hour at a time in the nets with a bowling machine and just trained myself to leave the ball. Some of them smashed into my stumps, but in the end I realised that if the ball went outside the line of my left eye (right eye for right-handers), then I could leave it. Practising to leave the ball in the nets gave me much more confidence to do the same out in the middle, and meant I was less prone to edging the ball to the slips.

Early on in an innings, most batsmen are a bit slow onto the ball, and their feet don't move properly. It took me three years in first-class cricket to learn the lesson that I had to bide my time before I went for more expansive shots. So nowadays part of my getting-in plan is always to leave fuller balls outside off stump. I can still score off shorter width, or wait for the bowlers to lose patience and come straighter. If they come too straight, and into my legs, as a left-hander, that gives me a better chance of getting the ball down to fine-leg.

EVADING THE BOUNCER

If you're facing a hostile fast bowler when you first come in to bat, you can be pretty sure that early on in your

When facing a bouncer, keep your eye on the ball for as long as possible.

innings he is going to test you with a short ball. Dealing with this threat is something you have to learn for yourself; no coaching manual can make you do it right, because the most important attribute you need is courage. But there are some key things I have learned to do to help me handle this situation.

The old adage of keeping your eye on the ball the whole time is easier said than done, but that's your aim. I would usually try to play the short ball if it's chest or shoulder height, but if it gets big on me or it's really quick, I try to evade it – it's amazing how quickly your body can move out of the way when it has to. My height helps me here, as a bowler would have to pitch it quite short to get it up at my throat, which wouldn't be the case for a shorter batsman. As a left-hander facing a right-arm-over bowler, I might sometimes get cramped up a little more than others, especially if the ball moves back into me, but even so the point remains that I try to watch it for as long as possible.

The other important aspect of playing short-pitched bowling is that you've got to be brave enough to wear a few, because you need to prefer to be hit on the shoulder than to fend it off with your gloves and get yourself out. It's a strange thing to tell your mind to do: leave the ball and take the hit, but you can do it. This is where the courage really comes in. You must also make sure that your bat and gloves are nowhere near the ball – whatever the cost in terms of pain. Note how in this picture my hands are a foot below the bounce of the ball, so there is no chance of me getting an edge.

Always keep the bat and gloves well below the bouncer to avoid any chance of giving a catch.

BACK-FOOT DEFENSIVE SHOT

If the ball hasn't bounced quite high enough to be considered a bouncer, then you can turn the tables on the bowler. The back-foot defensive shot is an easy way to pick up one in the covers. The important thing here is to play the ball close to your body; there's no point in reaching for it, as that increases the chances that you will edge it. If the delivery is any wider, either leave it or if you feel well-enough established you might as well play a full-blooded cut shot or punch shot, because I think it's criminal to nick a defensive shot when it's wide of the stumps.

This picture also illustrates how you need to play the ball under your nose, and how you should move your back foot across to off stump to cover the ball.

As with the previous shot, this photograph illustrates the importance of keeping your eye on the ball right until it hits the bat. There is no way I'm going to edge the ball here: my head's the right side of the ball to be able to watch it onto the bat, my hands are high, I'm off the ground and using my whole frame. By keeping my head slightly to the off side of the ball, I get a perfect view of it. If my head was to the on side, my gloves would obscure my view of the ball and there's more chance of getting an edge.

Everything looks under control in this back-foot defensive shot.

PLAYING THE BALL OFF YOUR RIBS

As a batsman, I am lucky that I can use my height and get on my tiptoes to ride the ball and guide it down to deep square-leg or fine-leg to rotate the strike. When you're new to the crease, there's one thing for sure: if you're facing a good quick bowler who's looking like taking wickets, you're safer at the other end.

Being a left-hander, I am used to getting a lot coming in to my ribs from those bowling right-arm over. So this is really a bread-and-butter shot for me, a way of releasing pressure and rotating the strike. Doing this can be really important, especially if I'm batting with a right-hander, because it will help to knock the bowler out of his rhythm, as he has to adjust his line each time we change ends. This sort of shot is also an effective way to keep the scoreboard ticking over in limited-overs cricket when there isn't a big shot on.

I've come back in my crease and made sure that I've got over the ball to play it safely down to fine-leg.

Guiding the ball down to third man in this way is a shot only to take on when the slip cordon is vacant.

STEERING DOWN TO THIRD MAN

Sometimes, you have to recognise that however much you want to play a big shot, the ball is simply not there to hit. A delivery that comes in at your chest, cramping you for room, is just such a ball. The best option, if you want to score off it, is to play it late and run it down to third man. It was a shot that Marcus Trescothick mastered in limited-overs cricket. Although it may have brought him only a single, it was a very effective option, because he made it so hard for a bowler to see how he could deliver a dot ball. In Test cricket, one would not normally try this shot, as there is usually a slip cordon waiting to pounce. This shot is strictly for the times when the slip area is vacant.

This is one of those rare occasions where I might alter my batting style between Test and limited-overs cricket, to reflect the field settings I'm confronted with. It is always something to bear in mind with any shot you take on: what is the value in playing it? And what are the risks?

The reason I don't greatly change my approach between the different formats is that in Tests I'm often sent in by Andrew Strauss with licence to go and score as many runs as I can when we're pressing for a declaration. So I'm usually looking to be as busy as I can and to manipulate the field. If I get to bat in limited-overs cricket, then that is an essential part of the role in any case.

THE BACK-FOOT PUNCH

Once I've got myself settled into my innings, built up a bit of a sweat, scored a few runs and got used to the pace of the pitch, I can look to accelerate my scoring by increasing the repertoire of shots I choose to play. For this shot, rather than simply defending the ball, as I would do at the beginning, I look to attack it.

I've picked the length and rocked back, trying to play it as late as possible, waiting for it to be right under my nose. The key to back-foot shots is playing the ball as late as possible and getting the timing right, as that's where you generate your power.

The back-foot punch is a good way to accelerate the rate of scoring once you've established yourself in your innings.

the summer of 2011, against India at Trent Bridge. We were struggling badly in our first innings, and the best response seemed to be to go for my shots. Fortunately, I got away with it and made a quick 64.

Going over the top isn't just about hitting it back over the bowler's head. If I get any width and I need to score a four, then I aim to go over extra-cover. If I don't quite get it right, the chances are it will still go flying over the slips in any case. This approach may not be how the top batsmen go about their work, but I think you should always play to what you know are your own strengths, even if it's not coaching-manual correct.

THE CUT SHOT

Every batsman has a favourite shot when it comes to scoring quickly, but I must admit this one is not top of my list, which is why it is probably another shot I won't play until I'm very settled in my innings.

I don't get too many opportunities to play the cut shot in international cricket.

The most important thing to remember is to use the depth of the crease when cutting the ball. Of course, you don't get many really loose balls in international cricket, but when you do get something that is short and wide, you can either roll your wrists over the shot, to play it down and square of the wicket, or else you can play it aerially down to the third-man area or backward point. Even though I'm deliberately hitting it uppishly, note how I've kept my head down, so I'm not losing control of the shot.

Although I've chosen to lift the ball in this cut shot, I've still kept my head down so I'm in control.

Chapter 3
PREPARATION

To be able to perform to the highest level when you travel abroad, you need to do all you can to get yourself ready.

As a member of the England squad, I spend most of my life away from home, whether I am touring a foreign country during the winter months, or travelling around the UK playing for England or Nottinghamshire. This means that going to a game fully prepared can become more difficult, as it is hard to create a settled routine when setting off from a different hotel or a different city every few days. Because of this, I have learned to develop various habits that will help to make me feel at home wherever I am in the world. As well as being mentally prepared, I also have to work at being physically prepared, so in this chapter I will explain some of the routines I go through to help ensure I am ready for action from the first ball of a match, whatever the circumstances or the location. There's no doubt that being well prepared for a game is vital, whether you are playing for your club side or going out to represent your country.

GETTING READY TO TRAVEL

If you're going to be able to perform to the highest level when you travel abroad, you need to do all you can to get yourself ready for what can be a very different experience to what you are leaving behind. There have been many well-known stories of players in the past who have struggled to cope with life on tour. There can be a whole range of reasons why: some have difficulties coping with the food on offer, especially in the subcontinent; some miss their families; some struggle to cope with the heat; and some just find the relentless cycle of travel, hotel, game, travel wears them out. The ECB has worked hard to help out the players on this, but I find that there is plenty I can do to help make my life as comfortable and as enjoyable as possible. After all, it's not as though we are slumming it – we get to stay in some superb hotels and are very well looked after wherever we go.

To help cope with any potential homesickness, I try to do everything in my power to make sure that my hotel room feels as much like home as possible, and have come up with a series of little ways to do that. Obviously, I don't have a wife and children at home, as some do, and that can make life on tour even more difficult for them – missing their family, and missing their kids growing up. But, just because there 's no other family in my house, this doesn't mean that I can't get homesick or that I won't struggle to settle into a new bed every few days.

To help with the latter problem, I take on tour with me a Molton Brown sleep spray. I spray this on my pillow in my hotel bed, so that wherever I go it always smells the same when I lie down. Having this simple familiar scent enables me to chill out and relax. When I'm moving about so much from hotel to hotel, it can make a big difference. As I live out of a suitcase on tour – I'm never in one place for more than a week, so there's no point in completely unpacking – it's important to have something that is always a constant.

For the same reason, I take Tetley teabags with me on tour. I will always have a cup of tea first thing in the morning. Then, I will also take a flask onto the coach with me, as sometimes the journey to the ground can last an hour. Again, it means that, wherever I am in the world, I can still stick to my preparation routines and have something familiar to hand. During those times when we're travelling to a game, I don't tend to plug myself into an iPod, as I'm not one who wants to shut himself off from everything that is going on around.

Having said that, I'm pleased we get our own hotel rooms, and don't have to share as used to be the case for England sides in days gone by. But that doesn't mean I want to be alone in there the whole time, and this is where the next essential item in my luggage comes into play. To help me while away the time, I take my Xbox with me. I will play *Call of Duty* or *FIFA* or something like that – team games are the best, as we will often end up with four or five of us in a room. Graeme Swann is my regular partner, while Jimmy Anderson and Tim Bresnan will often be our opponents. Eoin Morgan and Steve Finn are team-mates at Middlesex, so they often join up as a pair, too. Being able to have fun together like this can play a big part in keeping us

A cup of tea in my favourite Brian Clough mug. I always take some Tetley teabags with me on tour.

all happy, especially in the subcontinent, where it can be hard to leave the hotel because of the attention we get outside. This way we can easily kill two hours just having a bit of banter.

A lot of people might think we are being over-cautious by staying in our rooms. But sometimes it becomes almost essential that we do so. When I toured India for the first time with the England Test side in the winter of 2008-09, it was just after the Mumbai terrorist attacks. I think the fans there were just very appreciative of the efforts we'd made to go back, as there was a great deal of speculation and debate as to whether or not it was safe for us to return. But when we did, we had armed soldiers standing guard outside each of our rooms, and there were ferocious checks before we were even allowed in the hotels. In those circumstances, and because of the advice of our security team, it was impossible to go for a wander to catch some of the local sights, or to visit other restaurants outside our hotel. In that sense, it was quite an awkward and challenging tour. We lived in the hotels or on the cricket pitch – nowhere else.

So I remember how Matt Prior and I watched something like 60 DVDs in about three weeks during that tour. Each day had a pattern, if we weren't playing a Test. We would train from nine to noon at the local cricket ground, then we would come back to the hotel for lunch. Afterwards we would watch a film, then we'd watch another. Then we might order up some room service and sit through another film, before finally turning in for bed. Unsurprisingly, on that tour we actually wanted our training sessions to last all day if possible, just for the chance to get us out and about. It was a good job that it was a short trip, as if we'd had to do that for much longer, it would have driven us mad.

That tour had begun before the terrorist atrocity with the limited-overs series, and we'd left the Taj Hotel in Mumbai only a few days before it was attacked. We'd actually been eating in restaurants where now people were being shot and killed. The TV stations in India showed live

> **In those circumstances it was impossible to go for a wander to catch some of the local sights.**

and really quite graphic footage of what happened, so although we were quite a long way away from the city when it took place, we felt very close to it all. In this country, they would have edited out some of the scenes we saw on the news. So we watched some awful things that will stay with me for the rest of my life. We knew the true horror of what had happened, and shuddered at the thought that it might have been us caught up in the crossfire, especially as the terrorists seemed happy to target foreigners as well as everyone else.

Understandably in the circumstances, we came home for a few days to let the situation be resolved. When the Indian security forces finally sorted out everything, we had to consider whether we should go back for a rearranged tour. It was not an easy decision to make, especially after what we had seen on TV, but we took a lot of advice from our security people, and in the end the team agreed that we should return. I think it was the right decision. When we got back to India, our mentality wasn't really to view it so much as a cricket tour any more, but to see it as doing a job that had to get done. We certainly had a sense that our tour made India as a country feel better, after such horrors, and it was good to be a part of that. It's not often in a cricketer's life that you feel that simply by playing the sport you love that you are making some sort of statement beyond the game itself.

Despite that difficult tour, I love going to India. You can be sure there will be a packed and aggressive crowd watching. It may surprise some people that it can get so hostile there. In England, at grounds such as Lord's, most of the crowd are pure cricket fans, so if one of our opponents has taken a wicket, when he goes down to field at fine-leg, he will be applauded by the fans. Yet when I bowled Sachin Tendulkar in Bangalore, I was heavily booed when I went down to the boundary to field. Of course they are mad cricket fans there, but what they're really passionate about is India, so if you do

The 2008-09 tour of India was hugely challenging, because of the Mumbai terrorist attacks, but on the cricket field we could enjoy ourselves.

anything against their side, then they're not going to like you for it. I didn't feel threatened by their passion; I loved the fact that it was so pumped up and electric.

It wasn't always like that, though, for India has changed. In the old days, there were often occasions when the fans rioted, and that is thankfully much rarer now. But some of the guys have told me about a tour before I was in the side when they had a game at somewhere like Guwahati, a venue where they hadn't had an international game for about four years, and it got rained off. The players were locked in the changing room while outside the fans were absolutely furious that the game had been abandoned. Apparently it was a very worrying experience, but I've never felt threatened when I've been there – even after getting Sachin out.

Indeed, our decision to return to India after the Mumbai attacks seems to have guaranteed our popularity there. We found that when we played anyone but India during the World Cup, we had quite a few local fans backing us against our other opponents. But as soon as we came up against India, we were the enemy of the country. I got an idea of just how personally they felt it during the summer of 2011. When we were beating India, my Twitter feed was filled with angry messages every day from Indian fans. It got to the stage when I wouldn't go on it at all during Test matches because of what they were saying on there.

Even when the situation isn't so fraught as it was during that tour of India, there are other things I will pack in my suitcase to help occupy the time we have to spend in our rooms. I always take my cards and we will play poker – it isn't about winning big money, as we keep the stakes very low, but it allows us to have a bit of fun. Anyone who joins us has to have a poker name to come to the table. For example, I'm known as Stuart 'The Goose' Broad – because I

Our decision to return to India after the Mumbai attacks seems to have guaranteed our popularity there.

Whoever it was that suggested I got involved in some DIY in Chennai was making a big mistake.

> **Normally, it is possible to get out and about, which I think is so important, as you don't want your hotel to come to seem like a five-star prison.**

always live on the river. My Nottinghamshire and England team-mate Alex Hales is known as 'The Halestorm'. It is a strict rule of the game that we have to call each other by their poker name.

I also like to take some books with me on tour. My favourite reading matter is undoubtedly stories from the soldiers who have been in Afghanistan, Iraq and so on – military memoirs are truly inspirational, I find. I'm keen to read their accounts because I'm interested to learn and understand what these guys have done for our country, and what they are continuing to have to do.

I remember when we were on tour in Bangladesh in March 2010, the bed I was sleeping in was really uncomfortable. When I began to bowl the following morning, I felt very stiff and I was aching as I delivered the ball. Because I like to feel as comfortable as possible when I'm playing, at the time it seemed like a big thing and I could have become distracted by thinking about why everything wasn't perfect. But I happened to be reading one soldier's book and in there he wrote about how he had been sleeping on the floor for four months, getting RPGed and shelled on a regular basis by the enemy. It made me realise what a great life I have, and there are far worse things that could be happening to me than having to sleep in a slightly uncomfortable bed while representing my country. If ever I start feeling sorry for myself, these books help to ground me and give me a proper perspective on who is making real sacrifices and facing challenges on a daily basis that I can't even begin to imagine having to deal with.

Most tours, however, are not as challenging as that India trip in 2008-09. Normally, it is possible to get out and about, which I think is so important, as you don't want your hotel to come to seem like a five-star prison. I look back at the England football team's World Cup squad in South Africa in 2010, and they seemed to be on a permanent lockdown; they couldn't do anything. I think that can drive you a little bit mad, and I'm not sure it helps to get the best out of a team. Even if the hotel provides us with a team room, where we can play pool, table tennis and other games, there is still a sense that we need to get out of the hotel complex.

Of course we have to be sensible about what we do and where we go, as in some places there is a danger we might get mobbed and so possibly pick up an injury, or else if we ate in the wrong places we could get food poisoning. However, I do like to go out with a few mates to a restaurant, or to do something like that just to get away from the bubble of the hotel and the cricket. We do what we can to get out, and when we're out we always avoid cricket as a subject of conversation.

These days, especially on the longer tours, the question of when or whether the families arrive is still a big one. It is not so long ago that it would have been virtually unheard of for the families to join the players on tour. There is no doubt that their arrival changes the dynamics among the squad: we go from spending every minute of the tour with each other to barely seeing each other, except at the grounds, once the wives and girlfriends have arrived.

Although I am one of the few members of the current England squad who doesn't have a wife and family, I recognise that their arrival has such a positive effect on the guys that I'm not a believer in keeping them from joining us. We spend so long away from home – I think I spent 280 days in a hotel last year – that you can't expect people not to see their families for that long and still want to give their all for their country for as long as possible. What better way to make a player feel at home (and so perform at his best) than having those from his home come to join him?

The ECB have been great at giving the families all the support they need when they come over. The only way I could see their arrival as being in any way detrimental is if the wives forgot that we're there to play cricket – we're not on holiday – and so that has to take priority over everything else. On the whole, I think they do realise that.

These days, especially on the longer tours, the question of when or whether the families arrive is still a big one.

GETTING FIT TO PLAY

Whether we are on tour or in the middle of a domestic season, there are a few basic exercises I like to do to maintain my fitness on a day-to-day basis. With my gym work, I don't want to push myself too hard or do too much, but I do need to keep my basic strength up. Like most county sides, we have a gym at the ground in Trent Bridge, which is set up with all the equipment we are likely to need to maximise our fitness for cricket. And it's important when doing any gym work to remember what it is you are trying to achieve by doing it. For example, I wouldn't do weights the day before a game, because I don't want to fatigue my muscles.

However, when I am doing weights, this is the sort of routine I will do (*right*). I've got 20kg in each hand, and I just lunge forward: I do ten on each leg, then have a break and do it again. In all, I will do three sets of ten. What is important in this exercise is not to let my front knee go over my front foot, and I also aim to keep my chest straight. In this way, I should end up with lots of right angles: my lower leg is on the vertical line, my upper leg horizontal and then my body is back on the vertical.

There is another exercise I do that is a really good one for bowlers. I take a 5kg medicine ball and then lie down flat with my arms stretched out over my head holding the ball. Then I do a sit-up and, as I come into the sitting

This exercise is a great one for bowlers to develop their core strength.

position, I bring my arms through and fling the ball at a partner, who is standing a few yards away ready to catch it. It's as if I were throwing in a football. He then throws it back to me while I'm still sitting or on my way back down. The reason I find this exercise so helpful is that it's great for developing whip through the body, and strengthening my push through in the delivery stride. As a fast bowler, this is what helps me develop and maintain my pace.

Keeping your balance while reaching to catch the ball is really quite tricky at first.

Another favourite exercise of mine is designed to help improve my balance. It is quite a tricky one to get right at first, but it is a very important one for me. As I run in to bowl, I have a split-second on my back foot before I whip through to deliver the ball, but if I'm unbalanced on my back foot it can unsettle my whole rhythm. So it's vital to get that balance right. I do this to work on my proprioception (a term we use to explain how we sense the different parts of our body working together to maximise our output and strength).

There are two ways of using the board. Sometimes I will try balancing on it on one foot with my eyes closed; alternatively, I will ask someone to throw a 1kg medicine ball at me. They can throw it in different directions, so that I'm constantly having to rebalance myself as I move to catch the ball. In order to do this, I have to keep my core tight, and the more I can keep my core tight, the more it helps my bowling as this begins to happen naturally during the game.

THE BUILD-UP TO A MATCH

As well as preparing myself both physically and mentally to be ready to go out to play, I have some specific things I do immediately before a Test starts. Having good feelings about a ground is something I find important to develop, especially if it is a new venue for me. So when we visit the stadium the day before a Test, I'll take the time to go and stand at the end of my run-up, visualise the ground full with a cheering crowd, imagine what it will be like, and then I mentally deliver my first ball. This helps me to feel at home in the ground, even if I've never played there.

When we go back to the hotel the night before the game starts, and it's time for bed, I continue with my routines to keep me prepared. This is always a horrible time because, as an opening bowler, I need to get ready for the day

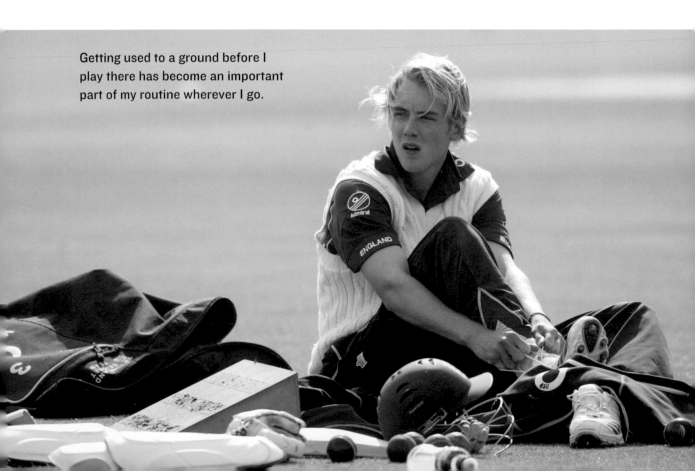

Getting used to a ground before I play there has become an important part of my routine wherever I go.

ahead, yet I don't know if I will be going to be straight into action or sitting back in the pavilion having a cup of tea when the game starts. It all depends on who wins the toss and what is decided then.

So I have to assume that I will be bowling first thing the next morning. In fact, I have the same routine before every game and every day's play. Twenty minutes before I go to sleep, I simply bowl some balls in my mind. The reason I find this helps is that it makes me feel like I've done it already when I go out to play, so I am much more relaxed.

The next morning, during the warm-up, the crowd begins to build up and starts buzzing; they are expecting us to perform well. This is when I begin to feel a bit nervous – it's good to have some nerves, as this gets the adrenaline going. I know that after that toss of a coin I'm either going to be bowling in front of millions of people judging my every move, or I'll be having a sit down and going to sleep in the pavilion. Cricket is very unusual in this way: a footballer or a golfer knows exactly when the action will start for him, but we don't, so we often have to build ourselves up only to find that we're doing nothing.

FINAL PREPARATIONS FOR ACTION

However great the outside pressure from the crowd may seem, it is nothing compared to the pressure I put myself under. As an opening bowler, I know I have to set the tone for the game, which creates a real tension. If I sat down and thought about it too much – how the way I perform at the beginning can have an influence on the whole Test match – it could become very worrying, but I have to take the responsibility for my performance. No one else can do it for me.

To get myself finally prepared to bowl that first ball, I go through a routine that settles me down. I walk back to my mark and begin by scratching it three times. Then I bowl three balls to mid-on or mid-off. Next I take a look outside the stadium, to take my mind briefly away from the arena and the intensity of the contest, to slow myself right down. I see it as taking myself outside the ring of fire. This takes the pressure off me: I'm not now thinking about how I have to set the tone for the entire Test match, instead I'm thinking that if I do my little routines, the ball will go where I want it to go. Then I jump up and down three times on the spot before setting off to run in.

I've always said that whether you're playing league cricket for your club on a Saturday afternoon or opening up at the MCG on Boxing Day, it doesn't change what you have to do in your job. Of course I have nerves when I'm bowling in front of a big crowd, but when I'm playing for England I know there are always many more watching on TV beyond those in the crowd. The crowd shouldn't affect my emotions when I come in to bowl; I should be able to shut them out.

These routines, or similar ones, can be used by anyone at any level of the game to make sure they start the game in a relaxed state of mind, focused simply on doing the job that they are meant to do. I've certainly found they have worked for me.

I'm in a slightly different situation when it comes to preparing to go out to bat. Coming in down the order, it is impossible to know when I will be called upon to go out to perform. This means I have to have a different level of intensity in my mental routines.

The way I get round this is I like to do things in a routine before I go into bat, so I create a mental rhythm for myself. I always put my kit on in the same order – pads, box, chestguard, armguard – then I sit down. I position my helmet to the left of me, with one glove on either side of it, and I have a can of Red Bull to hand.

I find somewhere in the changing room slightly away from the main buzz of conversation, where I can watch the cricket in real time and also keep an eye on the TV (where the volume is of course off). It's useful to be able to see the game in both ways: the TV replays can be helpful to see in detail what is going on, while watching the game live gives me a feel for the atmosphere. While I watch what's going on, I don't drain myself by watching too intently. Some of the other players have different ways of preparing themselves: Jonathan Trott

> **As an opening bowler, I know I have to set the tone for the game, which creates a real tension.**

doesn't watch the game at all, he'll just be playing strokes in the changing room, while KP is very relaxed before going in.

Once a wicket falls, I won't get up immediately, but first I'll put on my helmet and gloves, then I'll give them a tap and practise three forward defensives before setting off downstairs. On the way out, I usually have to walk through crowds in the pavilion and this can be a time when I really have to control myself. I remember in the Lord's Ashes Test in 2009, the MCC members were so close to me, with just a rope to make space for me to pass through, and there was a big cheer from them. Their support was so passionate that I almost had to calm myself down again when I got out.

At Trent Bridge, where I know many of the people in the pavilion, again I often have to regain my focus when I'm out on the pitch. It's not a question of shutting it out, because in England the fans are cheering me on, but I have to be quite selective about what message I take from the supporters. For example, once at The Oval I heard the crowd saying: 'Get stuck in!' There's nothing wrong with that, but my role then might have been to see us through to tea, and in an instance like that the crowd's suggestions for how I should play might run contrary to what we were planning to do. So I have to train myself not to listen to the words they say, but simply feel the support they are giving me.

Having gone through the crowd, I like to run over the boundary rope and take three sideways steps. When I'm halfway out to the middle, I like to stop and have a look around, see the crowds, look up at the sky and think: 'Right, this is the arena.' My approach is almost the opposite of when I'm bowling, as then I try to take my mind away from the intensity of the contest; as a batsman, however, I've been sitting in the pavilion, out of the action, but now I'm going into battle and I need to get the adrenaline flowing quickly. To do this, sometimes I might just stare at the wicket-keeper when I get to the crease – it's a way of getting myself up for the challenge.

My routine is slightly different in twenty20 cricket, as I have to be out in the middle within 90 seconds of a wicket falling, so I can't hang around. There's less of a problem getting that intensity, as when we're sitting in the

Sitting in the Trent Bridge changing room, ready for action.

dugout it is much easier to soak up the atmosphere than it is when we're in the changing room. Because of this, I've realised that I've got to keep hold of my emotions much more, because there's nothing worse than going out there, carried away with it all and forgetting my gameplan, and rushing into an ambitious shot and getting out.

Whether I'm preparing to bat or bowl, the key is to make sure that I am in the right frame of mind when I go into action, that the first ball goes where I plan it to, or that I'm ready to play the right shot to the first ball I receive. While this chapter has looked at mental preparation and doing the right sort of gym work, there are plenty of other things I can do to help ensure I perform to my potential, which is what we'll look at in the next chapter.

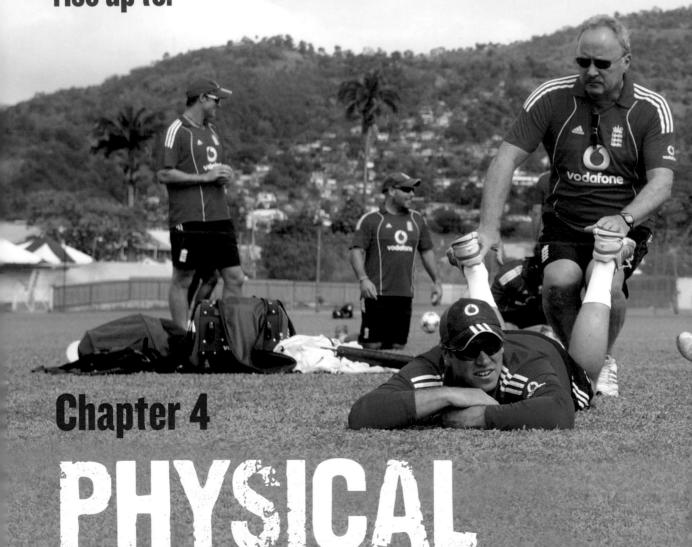

Having an injury can be incredibly frustrating, but I see this as just another challenge to rise up to.

Chapter 4

PHYSICAL

It is vital to do all that is possible to prepare the body for the stresses and strains that come with playing cricket.

While there is no doubt that getting yourself to feel mentally right to play is hugely important, it is also vital to do all that is possible to prepare the body for the stresses and strains that come with playing cricket. Also, as I've learned recently, sometimes your body can let you down, which means time away from the game. At any level of the game, having an injury can be incredibly frustrating, but I see this as just another challenge to rise up to. In this chapter, we will look at all the things you can do to help get yourself onto the cricket field in the best possible condition, and what to do when injury strikes.

DIET

People often ask me about the lunches and teas we have when we're playing for England. I guess it's a subject close to the heart of all cricketers. But the sad truth is that when we're playing a Test, we don't have some lavish spread laid out on white tablecloths, with uniformed staff on hand to serve out some exciting delicacies. The reality is much more mundane.

During a game, our lunches are prepared by the team nutritionist. If we're in the field and I'm going to have to bowl soon, I know I can't weigh myself down with too much food, so I will have a light lunch and a protein shake. It's slightly different in the subcontinent, where I used to struggle sometimes, because the lunches there would usually be curry, rice, naan bread and so on. Eating all that lot can get quite heavy, but having said that, when you're in a hot climate such as India, you also need to take on a lot of energy to cope. Getting the balance right between eating so much that I reduce my mobility while eating enough to keep up my energy levels can be tough.

In fact, the 40 minutes we have for lunch breaks can be surprisingly rushed. If we're in the field, I will often go straight to the changing room

An off-season lunch at the Larwood and Voce pub, close to Trent Bridge.

Fortunately, because we are burning so many calories when we're playing, I don't have to watch what I eat that closely to keep in shape.

and have a shower, then I'll get changed into some fresh kit, and suddenly 20 minutes have gone so there's not long left. Lunchtimes aren't a period when we just sit down, have a cheese sandwich and relax – it's business. We have to get what we need in that break and be ready for action.

If that is true of lunch, it is even more the case in the 20 minutes we have for the tea break. Usually, I'll just have a banana, a protein shake and I'm done. Sadly, there are no scones or anything like that on offer any more. That's why I love going back to my old club Egerton to sample local cricket teas where all the traditional favourites are available.

We spend so much time away with the team that our diet is often very structured. When we're playing, all our lunches are provided of course, and there's usually an evening meal at the ground, too, if we want it. Sometimes, however, we will eat back in our rooms at the hotel instead. Usually, the food on offer there is good quality, so we can eat well. Fortunately, because we are burning so many calories when we're playing, I don't have to watch what I eat that closely to keep in shape. And that means there is room for the occasional drink. Certainly, after a win I think it's really important for the whole team to get together and celebrate our victory with a beer or two and to enjoy the moment. It's what we have worked hard for, after all.

When I'm not with the England squad, there is a little more flexibility with what I eat. We are all given plenty of information on what foods are best for us, and which ones to try to avoid. However, there is no close monitoring of our diet: we are trusted to look after ourselves and to make sure that we keep ourselves in good condition. Generally, I try to avoid takeaways and the sort of rubbish food that we all know is bad for us. But beyond that I'll happily eat most things.

There was one exception to this, however, during the autumn of 2011 when I was recovering from an injury. I told the ECB that I wanted to use my time away from cricket to get as fit as I could – and they arranged a special diet for me. I was given just 2000 calories a day, and breakfast, lunch and dinner were delivered to my house every day. During that time, I trained really hard as well. In those four weeks I lost 1.5kg in weight and 24mm of fat around my stomach, which pleased me as I'm not someone who carries a lot of extra weight in any case.

The diet I was on went something like this: I would have a fruit granola for breakfast, followed by a protein bar in mid-morning. For lunch a typical meal might be a chicken and mango salad, which would be followed by a protein milkshake in mid-afternoon. For dinner, I'd eat something like beef stew. The difficult thing was that there were no cakes, chocolates or biscuits allowed. While there wasn't necessarily lots of it, the food was nutritious enough, and it is amazing to think how much you can eat with 2000 calories in a day – especially when you consider that a takeaway pizza can easily be 2000 calories on its own. It just goes to show how easy it is to eat more than we should. I'm not suggesting this diet would be appropriate for everyone. After all, I couldn't have got away with a diet like this if I had been playing cricket, as I need more energy than that to function at my best.

In terms of what I had to drink during my diet, I avoided fruit juice, because of the sugar, so I mostly drank water or tea. During that entire period, I couldn't go out for dinner or see my mates at a bar, because that would have messed up my regime. That was perhaps the hardest part of it all: having to say no to every invitation that involved food or drink.

So why did I volunteer to put myself through all of this? In the end, I think I did it almost as a challenge to myself. In the early stage of my recovery, I couldn't even bowl in the nets, and I knew I didn't have another game scheduled until January 2012, so I thought it was the sort of opportunity that wasn't likely to arise often. It's so rare for me to have such a long gap without bowling, so I went for it. I committed to it wholeheartedly, but after it was over I have to admit that that first bar of chocolate I had tasted phenomenal.

After a win I think it's really important for the team to get together and celebrate our victory with a beer or two and enjoy the moment.

(*Overleaf*) It's important to celebrate our successes, as here after England won the twenty20 World Cup in the Caribbean in 2010.

WARM-UPS AND RECOVERY

In the previous chapter, I explained how I get myself mentally prepared for action, but I also need to get myself physically prepared, too, and this involves plenty of work at the beginning and the end of the day. When I'm playing cricket for Nottinghamshire, I have a slightly different routine to the one I have during Test matches, when we need to be at the ground somewhat earlier. For a county game, I will tend to get to the ground about an hour before the start and spend a little while in the swimming pool, mostly to stretch my legs, back and hamstrings. I will usually swim a couple of lengths as well, but I won't do anything too vigorous. It's also a help that we have a gym in the ground, which enables me to do some work on getting loose before we start.

During a Test match the routine is slightly different. I'll get a call at 8am and spend a brief time in the jacuzzi to help get my muscles feeling warm and relaxed (I don't spend too long in there as it can also be dehydrating). After that, I'll go and have some breakfast.

When we arrive at the ground, the warm-ups before play are important to get me ready for action. But their real value is as a mental switch-on and they help me to tune in to my surroundings. One exercise I will often do is to bowl a few deliveries with a 1kg ball. I find this is useful, because it gets my muscles going and helps prepare me for action. So when I start to play for real, the ball is obviously

Bowling with a heavy ball is a useful warm-up exercise before play starts.

a great deal lighter. You might be surprised to learn that it doesn't destroy your rhythm, practising with such a heavy ball, but it does ensure your body is ready to go.

Another exercise I like to do during my warm-ups is to pull someone along while they pull back on an elastic band around my waist. I find that if I over-exercise in this way, then my body feels freer when I'm running without having to pull along an extra weight.

I also do a similar exercise with someone running alongside me, pulling me to one side. Or else, I can practise bowling a ball with them tugging away. This exercise helps develop and strengthen my core and trunk, as it makes it harder for me to stay upright and tall in my delivery stride. This really helps me to get my balance right as I come up to the crease when I'm bowling for real. If you do this exercise, you need to ensure that your partner is pulling hard enough that you have to tense your abs, but not so hard that you'll topple over.

Tim Boon helps me to warm up by pulling back on the elastic band, which makes me feel so much freer when I'm bowling.

As Tim tugs on the elastic band, I have to work harder to keep my balance as I deliver the ball – another very useful warm-up exercise.

This period before play starts is also a time when we discuss and finalise our plans for the day and focus on what each of us needs to do to help execute those plans. If we're back in the field for a second day, I tend to take these warm-ups quite gently as I want to ease my body back into the bowling routine without putting any undue stress on it or overtiring myself.

About 30 minutes before the start of play, I'll go back into the changing room to get my whites on. I'll then have a rub down, and about 15 minutes before play commences, I'll go out onto the pitch again to have a bowl. That way, when I bowl the first ball, it's as though I've already been in action for quarter of an hour, so I'm ready to go. In the old days, players used to warm up about 45 minutes before the start of play and then they went back in to the changing room to have a cup of tea or to relax, before they went out again when the match got under way.

In fact, it's only in the last a couple of years or so that we've changed our routine in this way: you'll usually see me out on the field doing a few minutes' bowling right up until the umpires are coming out. I take that as my cue to go back in, listen to a last few words from the captain and then I'm ready to go. This way, I'm already ticking and I've got a bit of a sweat on when I bowl my first ball.

I remember how I used to watch Mike Tyson coming out to box, and he was already sweating and looked completely ready for action as soon as the bell rang. That's what we want to achieve: a knockout blow from the off. These days, there's no space in first-class cricket for warm-up balls. If Jimmy Anderson has bowled a lovely first over, and I come in and get it all wrong to start with, then his good work is undone. This sort of physical preparation is not only about getting things right on a personal level but for the team as well.

After we have spent a day in the field during a Test, and when we know we've got to go out and field again the following day, the preparation for the day after begins the moment we come off the field. The first thing I do is to have a protein shake (this is something that the whole team will do, not just the bowlers).

Then, straight away, I like to get my boots off as quickly as possible, so that my feet can begin to recover from the day's efforts. I will then have a massage of my legs, especially my quads, so that they don't tighten up. After every day that I bowl, I like to have my sides rubbed, too. Ever since I tore my ab during the Ashes series of 2010-11, I've felt this is important to do. I suspect that the cause of that injury was probably because my ab had got a little too tight and I want to do all I can to avoid a repetition. This sort of tightness can come from anything – it can even be something as simple as sitting down for a long car journey. So I always have my abs rubbed through and extended after I've been bowling.

If I've had a good day and picked up a few wickets, I might be the one from the team who is selected to go and talk to the media about how the day has gone. This can take up to 40 minutes, but it isn't something I mind as usually when I've done it the mood has been largely positive. If I don't have to talk to the press, I will have hot and cold baths, which help relax the muscles and ensure that I am ready to perform again the following day. Fortunately, ice baths are no longer viewed as being an effective way to prepare, and so they have somewhat dropped out of fashion. I'm quite relieved about this, as I was never much of a fan of them in the first place!

People are often heard to complain that there's more support staff behind the England team than there are of us in the side. But I don't accept that criticism – I think they play a vital role in ensuring we can all play to the best of our ability, and they help minimise the risk of us picking up an injury that will keep us out of the action, or a niggle that might restrict our effectiveness.

I have to say that for a bowler, it's awesome to be able to walk off the field and have someone take me away to stretch off my quads. I know how much Matt Prior appreciates the fact that when he gets back to the changing room, there is a physio waiting to work on his fingers, which are inevitably battered and bruised after 90 overs in the field. Having this sort of help available is not an unnecessary luxury: being well prepared in this way can give us an extra edge. It gives us the best chance of keeping all the players fit.

We all have things we like to do after a day's play, but sometimes something comes along to upset that rhythm. Because I'm used to bowling about 20 overs in a day, I know what my body needs to help it to recover, and to keep it ticking over. However, when I scored my hundred against Pakistan at Lord's in 2010, I was batting for almost 300 balls and over seven hours, starting just after lunch on the second day and carrying on well into the third day. My next-longest Test innings was under three hours and just 132 balls, so the Pakistan innings was way beyond anything else I'd ever done.

I simply wasn't used to being bent over in my stance for so long. For a week after, my quads and hip flexors were so stiff I could barely move. I needed frequent massages in the following days to rub it all out. Batsmen can have similar difficulties when it comes to having to bowl longer spells. I remember after the first Test against Pakistan in Dubai in January this year, Jonathan Trott found himself running very stiffly after he had bowled just eight overs. He commented to me: 'Bowling's really hard work!' I could have said the same to him about batting after our partnership at Lord's. It just proves that your body gets used to whatever it is that you do, but it also made me aware that if I bat for a long time then I'm at quite a high risk of picking up an injury because my body isn't used to playing a long innings.

Celebrating reaching my century against Pakistan at Lord's – but the after-effects of such a long innings proved surprisingly painful.

INJURIES

Applauding the fans after England's innings victory at Adelaide in December 2010 – unfortunately by then I knew my tour was over.

Although I've picked up one or two injuries since the Ashes series in 2010-11, I would say that I have been pretty lucky on that score since I first played for England at the age of 20. I went more than four years without picking up an injury, which is quite unusual for a fast bowler. Since then, however, I have had four injuries, but if there is a positive to come out of it, they have at least helped me to understand my body better – and to listen to what it is telling me.

I noticed that in each case I'd had warning signs before the injuries happened, and realised that, perhaps because of my competitive nature, I'd put them to one side. If I can possibly help it, I don't want to miss a single match playing for England, and it is very hard to tell myself that I should rest rather than play, when all that is stopping me is the worry that something *might* go wrong.

My first serious injury came in the Ashes. It happened during the second Test in Adelaide. When I was bowling, I felt a little nick in my chest, almost like a stitch. I didn't think too much about it, so I kept bowling and then suddenly it went. It felt like an explosion inside me. But I still bowled another three balls to finish the over; I could hardly breathe by the end of the over, I was in so much pain. It was then I finally realised that I had to go off, and when I got back to the changing room and lifted my shirt, I was astonished to see so much blood under my skin, the bruising was that bad. I remember thinking to myself: 'What have I done here?' Even before I checked things with the medics, who confirmed that I'd torn my ab, I knew that my tour was over and this was a bad injury that would take plenty of time to recover from.

It was the fourth day of the match when it happened, and when I came in to the ground on the next morning, the manager told me that they'd booked me on a flight home that day. It was all so sudden: one day I was competing in one of the most important Test series of my career, and the next I was supposed to go home and leave it all behind. To be honest, I wasn't feeling ready to go home immediately.

One day I was competing in one of the most important Test series of my career, and the next I was supposed to go home and leave it all behind.

Fortunately, *Test Match Special* got in touch with me and asked if I'd like to work with them for the third Test in Perth. I have to say that softened the blow and allowed me to be psychologically ready to leave the tour. During the Test, in between commentary stints, I was able to go into the England dressing room on occasions, which made the departure more of a gradual break rather than a sudden wrench.

TMS's latest recruit tries his hand behind the microphone in Perth.

Working with the *TMS* team was a wonderful experience, despite the result of the game we were commentating on (England lost by 267 runs). It was fascinating to see how Jonathan Agnew, Christopher Martin-Jenkins, Michael Vaughan and the rest of the team explained what was going on, and how they conducted themselves on-air.

I remember Aggers talking about the birds flying across the outfield. Obviously, I could see what he was talking about, but I could just imagine being at home on a dark winter's night, listening to it and being transported to the ground by his words. The skill with which he did that was simply awesome.

My next injury came during the World Cup held in India, Bangladesh and Sri Lanka. The tournament started in February 2011, about ten weeks after I'd torn my ab. We were involved in a tight game in Chennai against South Africa, one that we needed to win after we had been surprisingly beaten by Ireland in our previous match. Having scored only 171, we had to fight hard to defend our total. I bowled a tight first spell, picking up a couple of wickets, but I began to feel uncomfortable and decided to come off the field. Suddenly I was struggling to move. However, I had to go back on to finish my allotted ten overs, and I even picked up a couple more wickets to help us win the game by just six runs.

I should have been thrilled, but when I came off at the end of the game, I recognised that something wasn't quite right, even if I didn't feel any great pain. Then I was picked out for a random drugs test, which meant I had to sit around for an hour after the game so I could provide a sample (it's always hard to do this after a game when you're dehydrated).

When I'd finally managed to give them what they needed, I came back into the dressing room to get changed. But when I tried to bend down to untie my shoes, I just couldn't do it. Eventually, it was discovered that I had broken my rib and my World Cup was over. There hadn't been any blow on it – it had broken simply from the impact of bowling. The pictures of me bowling that

I've just picked up another wicket against South Africa in the World Cup in March 2011. Astonishingly, I was bowling with a broken rib.

In great pain after tearing my lat during the last over of India's innings at Lord's in the summer of 2011.

day show what adrenaline can do to keep you going, but as soon as the adrenaline stopped, I couldn't move because of the pain. I'm still not sure if this injury was related to the previous one, but it was the same side, so it is possible there may have been some link between the two.

Unfortunately, it wasn't long before I picked up a third injury. This one came at the end of the summer of 2011. I'd bowled more than 150 overs during the Test series against India, and this was followed by the one-day internationals. We had back-to-back games at The Oval on the Friday and Lord's on the Sunday. When I was warming up for the second game, I felt pretty average, and thought something didn't seem quite right.

Coach Andy Flower checked to see if I was OK, and I told him that I was. However, because I was a little worried, I decided to bowl within myself during the game, just in case there was something wrong. I got through it all right, until I had to bowl the last over. Unfortunately, M.S.Dhoni hit me for six, and I decided I had to fire in a yorker so as not to let things slip at the end. Immediately after bowling my effort ball, my hand had excruciating pins and needles shooting through it.

I knew that I had a major problem, and it was discovered later that I had torn my lat (the word is derived from the Latin for 'broad', which might have brought an ironic smile to my face had it not hurt so much).

My fourth injury on this bad run occurred in Sri Lanka in March this year, but it came about because of a freak

The key afterwards was to realise that I'd bowled those no-balls because of a specific problem I had then.

accident, rather than through the day-to-day stresses and strains of bowling. What happened was this: during a warm-up game before the first Test, a ball was skied up to me. As I ran round to catch it, I landed on the boundary rope and strained my ankle ligaments.

That niggle caused me to run differently when I was coming in to bowl, because I was trying to protect my ankle, and that ended up giving me a calf strain during the first Test. It wasn't a major problem, but it meant that I missed the next Test and came home. Because it was only a short series in any case, there was no need to remain out there. In some ways, this one was the most frustrating of all my injuries, because you train as hard as you can to be ready for a Test match, then you trip over a rope and all the work is wasted.

Although I played in that first Test, I could tell that I wasn't right, because my stride pattern was so far out in my run-up that I kept on bowling no-balls – there must have been eight in all – and normally I very rarely bowl any. Sadly, with one of them, I had Prasanna Jayawardena caught and bowled. Sri Lanka's wicket-keeper had been leading a tail-end recovery, and at the time our target was 293. Had he been out, it would have been the end of their innings, but they went on to set us a total of 340 to chase. Although we lost the game by 75 runs, I do wonder if that error might have cost us the game.

I don't know what else I could have done to help get me through that Test; I'd strapped up my sore ankle and it seemed all right to bowl on. But in the end, as a bowler, rhythm is everything and I lost it in that Test. The key afterwards was to realise that I'd bowled those no-balls because of a specific problem I had then, and not to start worrying that I had a more general problem with no-balls when I run in, as that would distract me from focusing on my job.

AVOIDING AND RECOVERING FROM INJURY

After picking up three body injuries within a year, I tried to change my mindset. It made me realise that fast bowling is hard work and it is always going to bring with it the threat of picking up an injury. I've also learned to recognise that when I get those warning signs, as I did in each case, I must take notice of them and give myself the break my body clearly needs. There was an example of this after the three-Test series against Pakistan in the UAE in the winter of 2011-12, when I was rested for the warm-up game for the limited-overs international series, as it was felt I didn't need the extra work.

The physio pointed out that, including warm-up games and practice sessions, I had bowled something like 250 overs in January alone, which is a huge amount of work. When you consider that on the county circuit a fast bowler might bowl 600 overs in a season, Jimmy Anderson and I were bowling almost half of that in a month. It puts our workload into some sort of context, especially when you recognise the additional intensity of international cricket. But that's why Test cricket is so special: it pushes you to a higher level.

When they realised just how much we had done, the physio told me and Jimmy not only to miss the warm-up game but not to bowl at all for five days to give our bodies a chance to recover. In a previous era, we might not have had the break, and we could have picked up an injury. This sort of injury prevention simply wasn't around five or ten years ago.

This is why, on the whole, the England squad has been quite lucky with injuries, and there's no doubt how much we are helped by having such a great support team working with us. They do such a fantastic job for us. They are there to help make sure the players can perform, and they are constantly finding new ways to make sure we are in the best condition. For that series, we each wore a GPS monitor. Mine revealed that I was doing 17km in a day during a Test. I had no idea I was covering so much ground. I was not running for the entire time, of course, but the more data we get the better it is for us to understand what we need and when we ought to rest.

The way he copes with the normal wear and tear on his body is one reason why I have so much respect for someone like Sachin Tendulkar. Although he's a batsman, to play in almost 190 Tests is an unbelievable achievement (and that's not counting his world record of more than 460 one-day internationals). Then there was Courtney Walsh, who played in 132 Tests as a fast bowler – it's absolutely incredible. Although he didn't have the same amount of one-day cricket as we do now, he still bowled more than 5000 overs in Test cricket – by comparison, I reached just a third of that amount during the last summer.

I remember seeing Walsh in a hotel in London when I was playing at Lord's and I was properly starstruck. He was eating his breakfast, and I was simply in awe of him. He was one of those guys I'd grown up watching on TV, and I'd watched so many videos of him in action. He was the kind of bowler who had inspired me as a kid.

It's been a hard lesson to learn, saying no to playing, but I hope that I can keep heeding the messages I'm getting from my body and so not pick up an injury that I just might have been able to avoid. Of course I want to play every game, but if I can take a week's break to recover, in the long run I know I'll miss less cricket. To miss one game rather than ten has to be worthwhile.

Jimmy Anderson and I remind each other what a ball looks like after one of our periods of enforced rest to keep us fresh.

Even with an injury, there are ways of taking the positives from them.

I must admit, however, that that has not always been my view. When I was told by Andy Flower that they wanted to send me on a fitness training programme, and that I was going to have to miss the two Tests against Bangladesh in the early summer of 2010, I have to confess that I was annoyed about it. I want to play every Test I possibly can for my country.

Initially, I didn't react positively to the idea, but then Andy Flower explained his reasoning. He pointed out that I'd gone straight from school into first-class cricket, then from Leicestershire to playing for England. In all that time, I'd never had a period when I could build up my strength – it had all been about staying fit to play cricket. He felt I needed to get some extra strength into me, so that my body could withstand all the punishment it gets from bowling fast.

In that period away, I did a lot of work with weights and I'm sure it helped me. However, I would still say that I probably felt more benefit from my time in the autumn of 2011 when I was on my diet and doing a lot of physical gym work.

That said, I have to believe it is worthwhile if it can help me to stay fit. After all, injuries make me feel as low as I can go as a sportsman: I find myself watching my team-mates in action on TV when I want to be there with them. I will go to the gym to work on my rehab, which can be dull repetitive work, but I know that I have to stay positive about doing it, as that is what is going to get me back.

But no matter how focused I am on my task, events can still conspire to bring me down: I remember the time the guys were about to secure the Ashes in Sydney and I was running along the Trent in a temperature of −3°C. At the time they won it, I didn't even realise they had done so, because I felt so far out of the set-up. I came back home from my run and checked my phone and saw there were some texts on there. It was only then that I realised we had done it – but that was it. I was pleased, obviously, but I desperately wanted to be there, to be a part of what was a famous triumph, our first victory Down Under since 1986-87, all those years ago when my dad was playing.

However, what I've learned to do when I'm injured is to reset my mind. I recognise that it is unhelpful to be thinking: next week I was supposed to be in India playing in Mumbai. Instead, I have to concentrate on my own targets, not on what I would have been doing, but on what I *can* do. I have to think that next week I will be able to lift that weight, and set myself little goals on the road to my recovery. So my best advice if you have an injury is simply that: reset your goals to what you can do.

Even with an injury, there are ways of taking the positives from them. Each of those first three injuries kept me out of action for two months, but I was fortunate with the timing of some of them. For example, the lat injury meant I missed just five one-day games. If I'd picked up that injury in June, I could have missed most of a summer.

The other thing I've learned to do when I have an injury is to have something to look forward to. I followed Arsenal midfielder Jack Wilshere on Twitter during his injury that kept him out of action for a whole season, and he's obviously had low points where he's had setbacks. But interestingly, when he's had a problem, he's decided to take a break and go on holiday for a week to chill out and reset his targets so that he can start again, feeling ready to work on his recovery once more. The important thing to remember if you do have a setback is not simply to push harder to catch up with your original schedule, but to reset your goals and go again. For some it is worth taking a break from the game for a while to mentally freshen yourself up a little.

Injuries are any sportsperson's biggest fear, but despite my recent run of injuries, I don't actually feel that I have too much to worry about in a long-term sense. As I've said, I hate having to miss games through injury, but each of my injuries has had different causes. People quickly forget that I had several years without any troubles, which is unusual for a fast bowler, so it's not as though it's been a continuing problem. I know I'm in a daft sport for injuries, so I have to see them as an unpleasant and unwanted part of the job. But by doing my physical preparation the right way, and by getting to understand the messages my body is giving me, I can ensure that I miss as little cricket as possible. And that has to be one of the goals I set myself. As the next chapter will show, setting the right goals and how you go about achieving them is crucial to doing well on the cricket field.

Chapter 5

GOAL SETTING

There is no point in setting a goal for yourself if you don't also give plenty of thought on how you are going to get there.

Within the England team we often look at what goals we should be setting ourselves. Of course, it is the easiest thing for us to say 'We want to be the best Test side in the world' or for someone to set their own target to be the best in the world at what they do. However, coming up with the goals is not the important part of it – the crucial thing is what we do as a team, as individuals and in given situations to achieve those goals. There is no point in setting a goal for yourself if you don't also give plenty of thought on how you are going to get there. In this chapter, we'll look at some of the goals we have set out to attain – and, indeed, one goal that some have suggested I should be aiming for.

UP THE ORDER?

When I started out in Test cricket, my batting average was really quite good, at over 37. True, I was helped by some not-outs, but I also picked up three half-centuries in my first 12 innings, which was a very encouraging return. To be honest, I think the main reason I started so well in my Test career was because the wickets were so much better, and I found it was easier to play my strokes,

Hitting out during the 2009 Ashes series. Despite shots like this, I am happy with my position in the England batting line-up.

With Graeme Swann, my England and Nottinghamshire team-mate, who has helped
so much with the balance of the side.

even if the quality of the bowling I was facing was also of a higher standard.

Whatever the reason, there was a moment when Geoff Boycott was heard to compare me to Garry Sobers, which is about as high a compliment as one could get. When Sobers started in Test cricket, he actually batted at nine and then quickly moved up the order in subsequent Tests. And perhaps this was the reason why some people have asked me if I have ever targeted a higher batting position in the England line-up.

My goal is not to move up the order, but to be a number eight who delivers runs and can support whichever batsman is there with me.

I can honestly say that I don't feel I should be higher up the England batting order. I see my usual position as being number eight, though when Tim Bresnan plays I tend to drop down to nine. The reason it strikes me as being unlikely I'll go up the order is that we usually pick a side with six batsmen and Matt Prior at seven. He averages well over 40, and when you add his runs to a similarly prolific top order, almost all of whom also average over 40, this means we're usually putting a lot of runs on the board and creating scoreboard pressure.

The runs that they score mean that the need to have the fifth bowler, as we often did in the past, is largely gone. Remember, it is not so long ago that we had Freddy Flintoff batting at six and averaging 32; and when I started in the county game, Ashley Giles was England's regular number eight. He was viewed as a very useful batsman in that position, yet he averaged just over 20 and made only four fifties in his 54 Tests.

We set ourselves a target to reach 400 runs in our first innings. Then, knowing we have a great spinner in Graeme Swann (who can also contribute very handily with the bat), this means we can rotate our three seamers, keeping them fresh throughout the day. Australia supplied the template for how to make this work. Their success came around having Warne (also a very useful eight) working in combination with three seamers.

So my goal is not to move up the order, but to be a number eight who delivers runs and can support whichever batsman is there with me when I

These players have all been useful cogs in their team, and that is what I hope I am for England.

start – almost every time I come in to bat, there is someone at the other end who averages over 40.

If I have an ideal person to emulate as a number eight, it would be Shaun Pollock (who averaged 32 in his Test career). Wasim Akram was pretty useful too. Nowadays, I would say that Daniel Vettori is probably the best batsman in that role. All of them are guys who can score hundreds. I proved against Pakistan in 2010 that I can do this – now my goal is to do it more often.

These players have all been useful cogs in their team, and that is what I hope I am for England. What is more, the way Pollock and Akram batted was important too: they were aggressive and positive run-makers. We talk about this in the England changing room: we send in the top order to take the shine off the ball and to do the crucial but perhaps more boring role, then we have KP, Bell, Prior and so on to follow them – our batting line-up just explodes all the way down. With the batsmen we have, we can be 100 for two off 50 overs and yet still score 400 off 120 overs.

I must admit, I didn't always feel quite so useful in the England team. During my first dozen or so Tests, when Fred was still in the set-up, I felt as if I was barely used as a bowler. I'm not sure we needed five bowlers, so having me there was almost a luxury. It's fine to have someone like Shane Watson in Australia, or Jacques Kallis in South Africa, as a fifth bowler. They probably bowl only ten overs a day, but it works in the balance of their side, because their primary role is as a batsman who can provide some very decent overs, rather than being an out-and-out all-rounder.

That wasn't the case with me. I was a strike bowler and yet I tended to be used as the fourth seamer. I often found myself coming on when the ball was 60 overs old, which seemed pretty pointless at the time. I felt they could have had another batsman in the side scoring hundreds, rather than having me bowling lots of overs with an old ball. Having said that, even if I didn't feel the side was getting the best out of me at the time, I now recognise that I was gaining plenty of experience during this period. So when the likes of Fred, Steve

Harmison, Matthew Hoggard and Ryan Sidebottom left the England set-up, I had enough know-how to move into a more prominent role in our attack.

Although I don't take a lot of notice of my own statistics, I do recognise that I'm in a stats-based sport. So my aim is to get my bowling average below 30 and keep it there, while I hope I can move my batting average up to 30 and beyond. If I can achieve both of those things, and keep them there to the end of my career, I know I will have done well.

Celebrating a wicket in New Zealand in March 2008. That winter was my first in Test cricket, but I often felt a bit-part player with the ball.

RESETTING GOALS

Sometimes in cricket it is important to take a step back and assess what you are doing to see if it is working as well as it might. For me, there was one of those times during the summer of 2011. In the early part of the season, against Sri Lanka, I didn't have a great amount of success. In three Tests, I picked up just eight wickets at an average of almost 50. With England having numerous bowling options, some began to question whether I deserved my place in the side, especially after I was rested for one of the limited-overs games against them.

During that period, I came back to play at Trent Bridge for Nottinghamshire against Somerset. Trent Bridge is always a ground that encourages the bowler to pitch the ball up, as it will always tend to do more that way. I gained confidence from taking five wickets in the first innings and also noted that I had more luck when I pitched it slightly fuller. For England earlier on in the summer, I'd felt in good rhythm, and was bowling with pace and aggression. There was talk that I saw myself in the role of 'the enforcer' – the one who gets the batsman jumping around, avoiding bouncers, while perhaps overlooking the crucial part of actually taking wickets. I'm not sure it was quite like that. However, there is no doubt that if you bowl short of a length, if the ball does anything it may be more difficult to get a nick, either because the batsman has more time to adjust or because the ball has moved further, but if you pitch it up a bit more there is a greater chance it may take the edge.

However, it isn't as simple as thinking: if I pitch it up I will improve my chances of getting wickets. I also realised that I had to overcome a fear that I have. My problem is that I hate being hit down the ground, even though as a tall bowler that's actually quite hard for a batsman to do. However, I've learnt from watching Jimmy Anderson, who bowls such good lengths and isn't afraid of having people try to hit him, as he recognises that's how he takes his wickets.

Pausing to reflect during the early part of the summer of 2011 when things weren't really going according to plan.

In conversation with my dad. I'm so lucky having a father who has played international sport himself, as he can understand what I'm going through in difficult times.

Obviously, during that period, I had several people giving me lots of advice, but I have always found that the most important thing is for me to work things out for myself. I listened to what people had to say, hearing opinions from those I respected, and I took ideas from various sources. But in the end, no matter what anyone suggests, I had to buy into the solution and get there on my own. I'm the one who has to control my career.

To help give myself some extra protection if I was bowling a fuller length, and to avoid being hit past me, I realised I had to change my field settings. Previously, I had tended to start off with a very attacking field, as I felt that was what an aggressive strike bowler should do. However, at the start of a spell, and particularly in early season in England, I recognised that I ought to give myself a chance to grow into a spell by giving myself some protection. For example, I might take gully out and put him at cover instead.

It's all about getting into a spell – Ottis Gibson, who was the senior bowler when I started my career at Leicestershire and who now coaches the West Indies – always had a first ball and last ball policy. In other words, he stressed how important it was that you do not go for a boundary with your first ball or your last ball of an over. That's why I'll rarely float one up first ball to see if it will swing; instead, I'll look to bowl a dot ball. Obviously, I'd like to take a wicket with every ball I bowl, but in fact I have to build a plan to take a wicket.

I decided to focus on trying to start off by bowling five overs for just five runs. That was an idea that I picked up from Paul Franks and Mick Newell at Nottinghamshire, among others. Rather than thinking about how I needed to take wickets upfront, and that to do so required a huge slip cordon, I decided instead to try to create pressure on the batsman. If I can bowl some early maidens in my spell, then I will gain in confidence very quickly. By doing that, the batsman might just be forced into a rash shot having lost patience because he couldn't even find a way to push singles. This logic can apply at any level of the game: the best way to pick up wickets isn't necessarily by having very attacking fields. In club cricket, there are very few batsmen who show real patience, so building pressure on them is just as good a way to get them out.

Having taken that decision to make what, after all, was a relatively small adjustment to what I was doing, I was delighted with the results. Later that summer, against India, I took 25 wickets in four Tests at an average of under 14. Bowling slightly fuller also brought bowled and LBW into play, and nine of the wickets I picked up came that way, whereas I'd taken only one in that manner against Sri Lanka. By resetting my goals and rethinking what I was trying to achieve, I had managed to transform my results and so helped the team to do even better.

Celebrating one of seven wickets in the first Test against India, at Lord's in July 2011. A slight change to my plans brought greater success.

TAKING ON THE SPINNERS

In Chapter Two, we looked at various techniques for building an innings against fast bowling. But when the spinners come on, it is important to set the right goals for how you want to play them. We have been focusing on this a great deal of late in the England side, because we have not found it easy to come up with the right solutions, especially when it comes to limited-overs cricket.

One problem we discovered during the World Cup in 2011 was that we were occasionally getting bogged down by the spinners on subcontinental tracks and we struggled to rotate the strike, partly because we just don't face so many spinners in England. One of the most effective ways to play them is to hit the ball with soft hands, guiding it into the gaps, so the ball runs away gently to give you the chance to score a single, as the fielders can't come in too close, because it then becomes much easier to hit the ball past them. 'Soft hands' is a term that is used often, and what people mean by this is that if you push your hands out to the ball, naturally you will hit it harder. However, if you let the ball come to you and play it as close to you as possible, then that is playing with soft hands. It helps prevent giving a catch to anyone around the bat, because the ball drops to the ground after you've hit it, while if you guide it gently into the gaps, it is much harder for the fielders to prevent a single.

Against spin, the key is that you mustn't let the bowler get into a rhythm against you, so rotation of strike is vital. Speaking to Swanny, who I think is the best spin bowler in the world, he says that he loves being able to settle in and bowl at someone for an over or two. I think the best way to frustrate the bowler, or to earn a bad ball, is to rotate the strike by pushing for a single and looking to pick up three or four runs an over by doing that.

THE FINE SWEEP

If a spinner doesn't have someone on the 45, playing a fine sweep is one of my first options to score a single. The most important thing to note here is my head position. See how I am getting it low enough that I'm right over the ball and my head is forward over my front knee. Being tall, I can get my arms and legs close to the pitch of the ball. What I'm looking to do is guide it off the face of the bat; I'm not trying to put any real power into the shot. If the ball goes fine enough, I might just get four runs anyway, as the pace of the delivery will speed it on its way towards the boundary.

The most important thing to notice in this sweep shot is my head position, which is well forward and low down.

Although we thought we'd learned our lessons during the World Cup, against Pakistan in the UAE we still struggled. However, I don't think that showed we have a fundamental problem against spin in the subcontinent. In many ways, it was a freak series, as the wickets were so skiddy and the spinners put such pace on the ball we struggled to get to the pitch. Even when they dropped it slightly short, there was still a danger. If we went back to punch it away and missed, it would leave us vulnerable to being bowled or given out LBW (especially with the DRS system in place), whereas in England the same delivery would almost certainly bounce over the stumps, meaning it was a free hit.

The ball wasn't turning a huge amount, as it can do in India. But this didn't help us either; in India the ball can often do too much if it turns, whereas the Pakistan bowlers were getting very little spin. In the UAE, Pakistan had a good plan for taking on our batting. They bowled very straight at us and they had a lot of cover on the boundaries. This meant that although we could rotate strike by picking up singles, we couldn't easily establish the control and momentum that comes with hitting boundaries. Our downfall was probably a lack of patience. If we'd settled for pushing a couple of runs an over, we could have done well. Perhaps we got bored at not hitting boundaries, because in England it's much easier to hit fours.

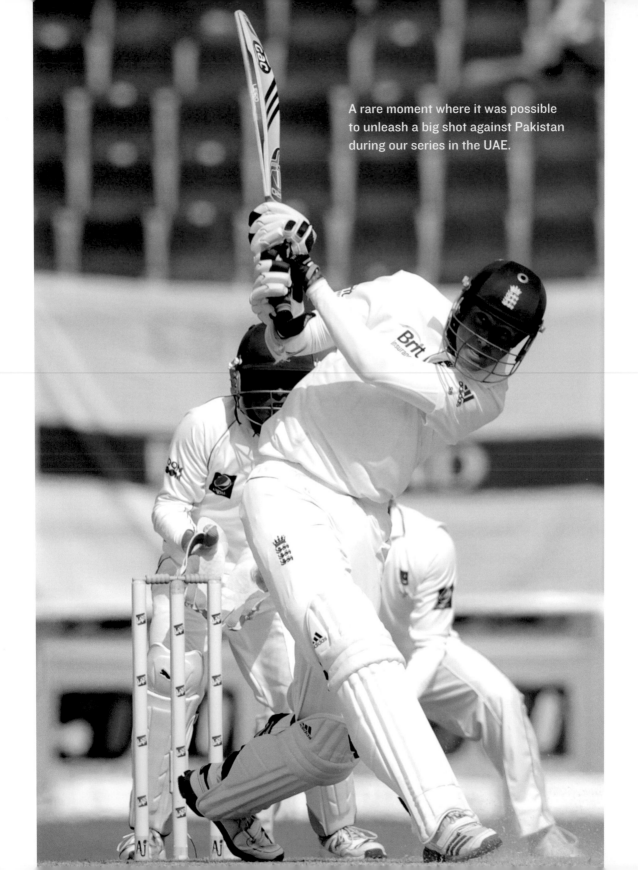

A rare moment where it was possible to unleash a big shot against Pakistan during our series in the UAE.

THE HARD SWEEP

As a number eight, I often come in to face spinners bowling at me with several fielders around the bat, so one of my aims is to try to clear some of them away. The hard sweep is a risky shot, so I don't bring my hands up high to play it – they go up only a little. The advantage of this is that if I see it's a quicker ball, I can pull out of the shot and still defend it; if my hands go too high, I won't get the bat there in time. Therefore, the power for this shot comes from below the elbow, with a big flick of the wrists; it mustn't come from the shoulders. See how my head is right down over the ball, which will help the ball go harder and along the deck.

In terms of which sweep shot is the right option to take, I'm guided by the field positions. If there's someone on the 45, there's little point trying the fine sweep, as that fielder will cut it off and prevent a single being scored. If I'm looking to hard sweep and it's a quicker ball, because my hands aren't high I can change my shot to a fine sweep. Equally, if I'm aiming to fine-sweep and

Note how in these pictures my hands don't go very high – the power comes from the wrists.

> # The key to hitting the ball over the top in the direction of long-off is to hit with the spin.

the bowler throws up a slower one outside off stump, I can change my shot as I have times to get my hands up and whip it away. The point here is that I try to delay committing too much to either version of the sweep until after the ball is delivered. It is important that I am able to adapt, and that I can have a Plan B if the shot I was aiming to play is no longer on. If there's no danger of an LBW, the other way to pull out of the shot is just to kick it away.

Any discussion of the sweep shot inevitably leads on to the reverse sweep. Although this shot is increasingly fashionable, especially in limited-overs cricket, I tend to avoid playing it. This is largely because I feel I have better ways of scoring runs, especially as I'm strong at hitting down the pitch. But I've worked on it in the nets, so if the circumstances were right I might use it. For anyone considering playing this shot, that is what I would advise: practise it in the nets for a long time before trying it in a match.

HITTING OVER THE TOP

The key to hitting the ball over the top in the direction of long-off is to hit with the spin. If a left-arm over spinner is turning it into me as a left-hander, this would be a highly risky shot. But if it is a right-arm round spinner turning it away from me, I can hit the ball with a full blade. What I aim to do is to hit it as straight as I can and, with the turn of the ball, it will naturally go more towards extra-cover. There is risk attached to aiming wider, as it involves making a late adjustment with your hands, but this is often where there is a gap, as fielders are usually out at long-off to cover

Hitting over mid-off is a shot I practise a great deal. Note how you can see the full face of the bat, and my head position gives me a clear view.

the straight drive rather than extra-cover. Note that my head position is just outside the bat, so I have a great view of the ball.

There's no doubt that this shot carries risks, so it is important when I take this one on that I have no doubts in my mind about it. It is worth practising this shot a great deal in the nets, as it will train your mind to know where the areas are you can do it most effectively. For example, if the ball is pitched a little bit short, it is harder to keep the shot under control than if it has been given a bit more air.

The other thing to remember is: don't try to belt it. When I play this shot, I'm not necessarily looking to hit a six, I'm just looking to clear mid-on or mid-off. I know that if I really catch it, it will go for six. I aim to get momentum into the shot, and once I've committed to it, I know I mustn't be scared of it or think of the possible risk. Indeed, here you can see that I'm slightly cramped up and not in the perfect position, but I've still committed to the shot.

Some might ask: why take the aerial route at all? It is always possible to beat mid-on by hitting the ball along the ground, of course, but I see hitting over the top as a positive way of dealing with the situation. If mid-on is up saving the single, it gives the bowler the message that he can't bowl to me there and he needs more protection in the deep. Once the fielder has been moved back, then I have an easy single instead. This picture shows my finishing position. Note how my head has stayed down even after the ball has gone.

There isn't a great deal of difference in how I play my shots over mid-on and mid-off. For me, the idea is to hit

Although I am slightly cramped here, hitting over mid-on, I have committed to the shot, which is vital.

the ball back over the bowler's head, but if it is spinning into me it ends up going more towards mid-on with a straight blade. I open up my front foot slightly to play to the onside, but I think the main difference between hitting to the on or the off is not with my foot position but with my hands. If I'm hitting over mid-off it's usually my top hand that's in control of the shot, whereas if I go over mid-on there is more of my bottom hand involved. If my bottom hand comes into play, it's crucial that it doesn't take over, as I still want to keep a straight blade.

Keep your head down when playing over the top.

COMING DOWN THE WICKET

Some people, such as Michael Clarke and many of the top Indian batsmen, are really good at doing this. Because I'm a tall guy I've less need to do it as I have a long reach. However, sometimes I will do it to try to unsettle bowlers who are bowling a good length. Having said that, even though he has a similar reach to me, Kevin Pietersen comes down the pitch to spinners quite often. But he's a top-order batsman and he is all about unsettling the bowler whenever he can. By contrast, Andrew Strauss, with a much shorter reach than KP or me, still rarely comes down the wicket as he prefers to take other options to score runs.

If I dance down the wicket I can simply push the ball to long-on, or if it's just right for me, I can hit through it for four. The key to this shot is that I try to keep my eyes level as I am on my way down. A good way to think about it is to imagine balancing something on your head as you move into position. I also try to click my heels together as I come down the pitch, so my feet don't get tangled up. Quick footwork is vital, as I don't want my feet to be still moving when I hit the ball; I want to have a solid base to work from on impact.

In the picture, note how my feet aren't crossed, and how I've come down the pitch in a straight line, which allows me to hit straight – though obviously I don't want to go completely straight because the bowler will stop it. You can see how the blade is aimed slightly to mid-on. Coming down the track like this always carries a risk, so I play it only when I'm sure there's a reward in it for me.

Coming down the wicket, my head is still and my eyes are level.

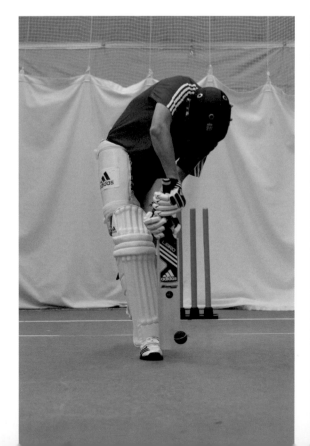

PUSHING INTO THE COVERS

When I come in to bat, I'll often find that someone is close in at short leg, but that usually means there will be a gap in the covers. As with the previous shot, the key is starting from a good base. Note how I am bending my front knee and using soft hands to push it for a safe single, hitting it just 20 yards or so into space.

What I focus on when I take my guard and look around me is not where the fielders are, but where the gaps are. So with this shot you are aiming to find a gap, and you can see how I've opened the blade to do so. By looking at the gaps, I'm programming my mind to look at where the runs are, not where they aren't.

While I'm waiting to bat, this is one of the things that I think about: for example, if there's a left-hander at extra-cover, there will probably be a run to his right hand; if there's a brilliant fielder at point, I know that I'll have to wait until the ball's beaten him before I set off. By looking at the field placings and what the fielders do before I get out into the middle, I can make sure that I am ready to run as soon as I hit the ball in the right place.

A good training exercise to work on this is to play tip and run, as it will show how hard it is to pick up the ball and throw it quickly enough to stop a single, if the batsmen set off straight away. Indeed, this exercise helps fielders just as much as the batsmen.

Soft hands are the key when pushing the ball into the covers.

DRIVING TO THE BOUNDARY

This delivery has a little more width on it and is full enough to drive, so there's no real risk in taking on the shot. As ever, make sure that you get your head right over the ball and hit it hard.

MAKING ROOM

If you watch top-class batsmen in action, you will notice that many of them move around the crease (especially in the shorter forms of the game) to try to create space to play a shot. Doing this can also be another way to unsettle the bowler, as he may be unsure where he ought to bowl. It is vital when doing this not to move too far – moving a foot to the off or to the leg is plenty. It's criminal to move right across your stumps and get bowled behind your legs, or to move to leg and miss a ball outside the off stump. In the England camp, we talk about the importance of moving early, so that we have a steady base from which to play our shot.

Getting these things right in the middle, however, can only come with lots of practice. So in the next chapter we will look at how to practise well and to make sure that the work you do in the nets gives the maximum benefit when you go out to play in a game.

With the ball a little wider here, I can hit through it.

Chapter 6

PRACTISING

By focusing on certain things, I can make sure that every ball I bowl or every shot I play in the nets is helping me achieve more on the pitch.

People know that practice is important in enabling cricketers to improve their game – the famous quote, usually attributed to Gary Player, about 'the more I practise the luckier I get' obviously holds true. However, I would slightly take issue with that as far as cricket is concerned. It's not simply the quantity of practice that makes a better player – *quality* of practice is just as important, too. When I go into the nets to practise, I do it with specific aims in mind. By focusing on certain things, I can make sure that every ball I bowl or every shot I play in the nets is helping me achieve more on the pitch.

For example, in the days before a Test match, the England squad obviously have some net sessions and I like to put these to proper use. So, early last summer, during the series against West Indies, if I was bowling at Andrew Strauss or Alastair Cook in the nets, I was actually executing my plans for bowling at Shivnarine Chanderpaul, rather than thinking about how I'd normally bowl against my team-mates. This was the most effective way for me to train in the nets. So in this chapter, we will look at how to make the most out of practice sessions, and how to prepare for unfamiliar conditions.

One thing I should mention now is that there is little point in doing things in the nets that won't work the same way when you try them in the middle. For example, especially at club level, I have often seen bowlers pinging the ball down to bowl bouncers in indoor nets or on concrete outdoor nets at the start of the season, yet the wickets in the middle are usually still relatively soft, so the same delivery would be easily put away in a match situation.

At that time of the season, the bowler should be working on keeping it pitched up, as that is what will be required in a game. Similarly, batsmen should work on the shots that will be most effective in the middle.

PAKISTAN IN THE UAE

Before we went out play Pakistan in the UAE in January 2012, we had some idea of the sorts of challenges we would have to face, and we had worked on things before we set out. We believed we had done all the right preparation for what we thought we would face. However, once we got there, some of our plans were disrupted when we found out there were no nets at the grounds. This proved especially difficult for Jonathan Trott and Andrew Strauss, who both like to hit a lot of balls before they go out to bat. Because of this, we had to go back to basics: we sent down old-school underarms to the batsmen, who played their practice shots against the boundary boards. In England, at all the Test grounds apart from The Oval, where there's no indoor facilities we can use on a rainy day, we can have some practice knocks whatever the conditions. This can be a great help if we have a Test like the one this summer at Edgbaston when rain interrupted the game so much.

We had gone out there expecting a lot of slow cricket in the UAE, as run-rates have traditionally been about 2.5 per over in Dubai and Abu Dhabi, whereas in England it would be more like 3.5. So I thought that I might bowl 25 overs in an innings and perhaps end up picking up two for 65. I told myself

Warming up on an exercise bike.

to recognise that if I did this I would have done a good job, as neither ground is particularly seamer-friendly. However, once we got there and saw how the wickets played, with a lower bounce than we had expected, the seam bowlers

The low bounce in the UAE made LBW shouts a much more regular option for me – five of my 13 wickets came that way.

decided to alter our lines slightly and we threatened the stumps a lot more. Given the spin-friendly conditions, if I'm honest, I think it was an excellent tour for the seamers: we got more out of the wicket than we'd expected and the Pakistan batsmen found us hard to cope with.

Our success came purely from the tight off-stump lines we bowled. The low bounce meant that whatever lengths we bowled, the ball wasn't often going

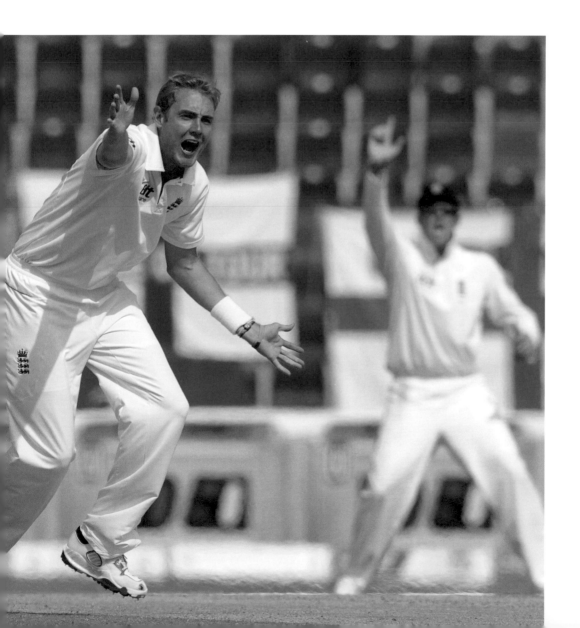

If your side is batting first on an away ground, watch how the home side organises its field placings in case you can learn from what they do.

over the stumps. It really helped me, at my height, to be able to target the stumps. In England, I have to bowl quite full if I'm going to have a chance of an LBW or hitting the stumps, and sometimes pitching it that full just makes it too easy for the batsmen to drive me. But what this experience showed is the importance of being able to adjust your approach and practise a new one when conditions prove different to what you expect or what you are used to. Adaptability in a bowler is a vital attribute to have.

We had expected to face a lot of spin from Pakistan. In Saeed Ajmal, they have one of the best spinners in the world, so we were prepared for that. However, what did take us by surprise was the extra pace that he and his fellow spinners bowled at. They were bowling 10kph quicker than our spinners, Graeme Swann and Monty Panesar. Unsurprisingly at that pace, they were not turning it a great deal, but they were very accurate, so it always felt that if you missed the ball they would get you out, especially as the low bounce meant the ball never seemed to go over the stumps. No wonder that, with spinners and seamers both targeting the stumps relentlessly, the series threw up a record number of LBW victims.

The lack of proper net facilities arguably hindered the way we were able to practise to counteract this strategy from their spinners. The way I tried to combat the threat, as a 6ft 6in player, was to get a big stride in and to get my front foot outside the line of off stump, so that if I was caught on the pad while playing a shot I couldn't be given out LBW. But in general, we probably have to hold our hands up and admit that we didn't learn quickly enough. Perhaps our best option would have been to get our bats in front of our pads to the straight ball to minimise the risk of LBW, but that would have reduced our scoring options. Trying to find an answer to their spinners was without doubt one of the toughest challenges this England side has faced in my time.

There was another change that I made to cope with the lower bounce, and that related to my hand position when holding the bat. In English conditions,

My hand position on the bat is lower (*right*) in subcontinental conditions than it is in England.

I tend to have my hands a little higher on the handle, because the bounce is a bit higher and you need to be able to adapt to it; in the subcontinent and in the UAE, I'd put my hands lower, as there's not enough pace and bounce to trouble me. The important thing is that you have to cover your stumps.

In terms of my own bowling, I decided to continue with the idea of giving myself some protection when bowling a fuller length by having a cover (instead of a gully) to keep the scoring rate down. I did a bit of work on it in practice, which meant I could concentrate on putting together dot balls and maidens. There was still the option, when it all settled down, to move cover back in at gully. This was a lesson one of England's coaches, Mushtaq Ahmed, had taught me was especially important in these conditions: build up into your spell. Build pressure by starting with some tidy overs; don't give them three overs for 15, because then you're chasing the game.

Another issue that arose during that tour was that subcontinental cricketers are very good at just running the ball fine through the slip region and picking up four runs. However, when we tried to play the same stroke, we found that they had closed off that option to us by placing someone fine at third-man, so we could score only a single with the same stroke. Therefore, if we wanted to get four, we had to play a bigger shot, rather than simply letting the ball do the work, as they did. So we learned from their field placings and adapted them as our own. This is something to look out for in any match: if your side is batting first on an away ground, watch how the home side organises its field placings in case you can learn from what they do, as they will have greater knowledge of where the ball tends to go on their field.

EXPERIMENTING

Any cricketer worth his salt will always want to keep on enhancing his game, whether it is improving a particular shot or developing a new delivery. Of course, I'd never try anything new in a Test or a major game; I always work on a new type of delivery in the nets first. It can take weeks rather than months to get something right in practice – though obviously as a professional I have the advantage of doing a lot of training.

The moment I know I'm ready to take something new out into the middle comes only when the feeling of it is right. You might try something for three or four days and find it frustrating as you keep getting it wrong. But I'm a big believer in the idea that you've got to get things wrong first so you can understand how to get them right. If a new delivery is regularly ending up going down the leg side, I will ask myself: why is the ball ending up there? Maybe I'm falling away a bit as I deliver the ball? The more I can keep an open mind about what is going wrong, the easier it is to find a solution.

People may respond that it is easier for me to put things right in the nets, because there might be video analysis available, or expert coaches who can spot small things that can make a difference. And it's true, I do have all of that available to me, but in the end I tend to work things out by how it is feeling: I feel how the ball is coming out of my fingers; I feel how my front arm is. I will use videos or input from a coach as well, but this is more as a back-up to my own feelings, rather than necessarily deciding things for me. It reinforces my own instinct.

Very early in my career, I understood how important it was to feel confident enough to try something out in the nets. I'd read something written by someone I respected so much, Glenn McGrath, who stressed that experimentation was

The nets are the best place is
experiment with a new delivery.

a great way to improve your game. In the same way, I hope that a 16-year-old kid, or anyone else, might see something in this book and feel 'I'm going to try that out tomorrow.' I see no problem with someone who uses the nets as an opportunity for trial and error. It doesn't matter if it all goes wrong there, either. I hate it when I see people beat themselves up after they've had a bad day. But in fact, you can learn so much more from your mistakes, so you can turn what seems to be a disaster into an opportunity. That's true in any walk of life. Obviously, if you keep on making the same mistake, it can become an issue, but don't give up easily. As a cricketer, you'll always look back on your good days with fondness, but in reality it's the bad days that make you who you are.

BOWLING VARIATIONS

One of the things that video analysis can do – and television can often illustrate this so well – is show exactly how a bowler holds the ball for certain deliveries. In the end, however, there are only so many things a bowler can do with the ball, and these are the options I tend to use most often.

To bowl my away swinger, I hold the ball slightly across the seam, which is aimed towards first slip. My middle finger is the one that controls the seam here – I can almost feel tiny palpitations going through that finger as I deliver the ball. Note how my thumb position at the bottom of the ball reflects the position of my forefinger at the top. When I'm delivering the ball, my grip is relatively loose – you should be able to move your wrist around a bit rather than having it completely tense.

For the inswinger, I turn the ball around so that the shine is now on the left-hand side. With this delivery, the middle finger is less important, but the index finger takes control, and I aim the seam almost to leg slip. I don't change my release position or my action to bowl this ball – it's purely about my grip. If you think about it, the pressure from your controlling finger is almost pushing the ball in the direction you want it to swing.

(*Left to right*) My grips for the outswinger, inswinger and the wobble seam delivery.

Sometimes, as a bowler, it's not about getting the perfect inswinger or outswinger, but about trying to wobble the seam a little. Curtly Ambrose and Courtney Walsh used to use this delivery very effectively. I tend to try this option this on flat wickets when the ball is not swinging. I hold it dead straight on the seam and just move my thumb across to the other side of the seam, so the ball feels a little bit less steady in my hand. Because my grip feels less secure, I often hold my wrist a little tighter to bowl this ball.

Because of that, it took months of practice in the nets before I felt comfortable enough to bowl this delivery in a Test. Indeed, it is a ball I've been bowling for only the last year or so, since I was confident enough to be sure I would get it right. It doesn't feel as natural in the hand as either of the swing grips, but that's what I'm looking for. I want the ball to do something unnatural and unexpected. I'm trying deliberately to get away from having the perfect seam position, so that with the wobble it might just nip back off the pitch, as I wouldn't expect it to do anything through the air. The two bowleds I got in Abu Dhabi, to dismiss Azhar Ali and Younus Khan, were both as a result of this delivery. In those conditions, to have this extra weapon available to me is a great bonus.

Another option I sometimes take on a flat wicket is to hold the ball across the seam. This is a really scrambled seam: as the ball goes through the air, it will look ugly to the cameras, but more importantly the batsman will see

(*Overleaf*) Months of work went into getting the wobble seam delivery right. To pick up two wickets in a day with it against Pakistan was a great result.

Holding the ball across the seam can put doubt in the mind of a batsman, and can be an effective way of bowling a bouncer.

something different and not be sure what to expect when the ball bounces. Anything I can do to create uncertainty when the conditions are against me has to be a good thing.

Holding the ball right across the seam is something I sometimes do when I'm bowling a bouncer. By holding it this way, if it lands on the leather it might skid on a bit, while if it hits the seam it might bounce more steeply. What I'm trying to do is to make the ball come through to the batsman at varying heights and paces. Just like the last delivery, this can help to create uncertainty at a time when the batsman may feel very comfortable in what he is doing. There is a downside, however, to bowling this ball, as it can quickly increase the wear on the ball. Because of this, I tend to use it more in one-day cricket, where you don't need to protect the condition of the ball to the same degree.

But if there is one delivery in a pace bowler's armoury that causes more discussion than any other, it has to be reverse swing. The idea here is to keep both sides of the ball dry. As the ball gets older, one side naturally roughens up, while the other side is kept as shiny as possible. Within the England team, we will often get Alastair Cook to do much of the work on the ball, as he doesn't seem to sweat, so he helps keep the ball dry as well. Ideally, the shiny side needs to be as smooth and baby soft as possible, which means putting in a lot of hard work on the ball.

It usually takes until the ball is 50 or 60 overs old before it will start to reverse swing. And even then, it may not happen. I do also wonder if it may just be that the quality of the balls we use in top-class cricket enables us to shine them up so well that we can get reverse swing, as I haven't seen anyone doing it in club cricket. That said, most club cricket games don't go on long enough for reverse swing to come into play.

When I'm about to start bowling, I jump up and down three times to fire up my knees and legs.

HOW I BOWL

I have a set routine when it comes to bowling my first spell, beginning with how I mark out my run-up. What I do is this: I walk 16 paces and then mark out three scratches with my foot, before bowling three balls to mid-on or mid-off. Unfortunately, because of the pace of a twenty20 game, there isn't time to do this, so instead I close my eyes and bowl the deliveries in my mind to retain my routine. Once I've done that, I will then jump on the spot three times to fire up my knees and legs. I start my run-up from perhaps five yards further back than my mark, and it is there that my right foot lands as I start to generate the real momentum as I accelerate up to the wicket.

In my delivery stride you can see that my front knee is braced, which helps me generate a lot of power and pace. For many bowlers, if you look closely, their front knee is bent, which not only puts a lot of stress on it, but also reduces their height at delivery. By keeping my knee braced, I can get the full

benefit of my height. I also try to get in as close to the stumps as possible when I bowl, as a wicket-to-wicket line pressurises the batsman to play at more deliveries.

When I bowl I take off from alongside the umpire, so sometimes I have to ask them to move back a little, and they're almost all happy to do that. I know that if I jump from level with the umpire, I should always land in the right spot. This technique has stood me in good stead, as I've rarely had a problem with no-balls. If I did have a problem, I'd ask the umpire to move back slightly, I wouldn't try to alter anything else.

Bowling no-balls in limited-overs internationals has become a complete no-no. With the advent of free hits for the opposition if you overstep, bowling a no-ball can be even more costly than it has been in the past. Especially in twenty20 cricket, it can really hurt you. I remember how Umar Gul bowled two consecutive no-balls against us in the UAE and it helped give us vital momentum in a tight run-chase.

If you don't prepare for the game mentally, and turn up with your mind focused on the task ahead, then all that work can easily go to waste.

Chapter 7

MENTAL

There are various techniques that I use to ensure that when I go out to bowl I am in the best possible state of mind before I start.

As a cricketer, you can do all the physical preparation for a match that you want, but if you don't prepare for the game mentally, and turn up with your mind focused on the task ahead, then all that work can easily go to waste. Whether you are bowling or batting, being in the right frame of mind is vitally important, especially as you can be sure that your opponents will try any tricks they can to get inside your head and stop you from doing what it was that you set out to do. So in this chapter, we will look at the things I do to mentally prepare for a game and how you can use some of the same tricks to ready yourself for action.

BOWLING IN THE RIGHT FRAME OF MIND

There are various techniques that I use to ensure that when I go out to bowl I am in the best possible state of mind before I start. Although I am not a great believer in video analysis, I do use video footage to boost my self-confidence. So, before I go on tour I'll get a package put together of me taking wickets. Watching myself sending the wickets flying everywhere and top batsmen continually giving away catches off my bowling is a brilliant way to put myself in a great frame of mind. This montage of seemingly hapless victims, all of them apparently out first ball, makes me feel almost unstoppable. Furthermore, this sort of positive visualisation reinforces

good habits and good feelings. I'm watching myself in action when everything goes right.

Beyond that, I've already talked about how I will go to the end of my run-ups the day before a Test and imagine bowling in front of a crowd and the television cameras, and how, when I go to bed, I will visualise the first few balls I will bowl the next day. By doing these things, I make sure I am mentally ready for action as soon as the game starts. This helps to keep me focused and calm.

Some may point out that this hasn't always been the way with me, and that I have occasionally lost my temper during matches, especially when bowling. I have to hold my hands up and admit that I had a few disciplinary problems earlier in my career, but I am pleased to say there have been fewer issues recently. The reason why I did occasionally go too far was that I used to get so into the battle that I'd forget where I was. This led to one or two incidents where I know I let myself down, and didn't help my team-mates.

Perhaps the most costly occasion was when I was once fined £6000 for throwing the ball at the Pakistan wicket-keeper, Zulqarnain Haider, when he was batting against England in the Edgbaston Test in 2010. That wasn't a good afternoon. In my defence, I have to say that I didn't deliberately target him. What happened was that, at the end of the over, we always throw the ball to Matt Prior and when I did this it hit him on the shoulder by mistake. I wasn't fined for the throw itself, but for the lack of a genuine apology. I was frustrated at the time, as he'd edged me for four a couple of times, but I recognise that I fell a long way short of how I should have behaved. I know there are many people watching whenever England are in action, and that it is important to set a good example.

I have worked with a sports psychologist to ensure that I don't give in to those moments of temper now; they don't get you anywhere, after all. The work we have done has paid dividends so far, even under the most challenging conditions. For example, the heat in somewhere like Sri Lanka can make it feel

Trouble looms. I've just thrown the ball and hit Zulqarnain Haider by mistake, but my reaction was to cost me £6000.

like you're in a cauldron, and your head is almost exploding, so that's when having a good temperament can really help. There was a quote from Lawrence Dallaglio that I often think about in those situations and that for me sums up precisely the attitude that I want to convey: fire in the heart, ice in the mind.

So now, if I feel the steam beginning to rise, especially when I'm captain of the twenty20 side, I'll look up into the air, over the top of the stands, and focus on something else for a moment. Doing that gets me out of the ring of fire and away from the contest. On these occasions, you might notice as I'm walking back to my mark that I'm looking up and above the pressure cooker. It completely chills me out, so that by the time I'm running in to bowl my next ball I've got my focus back. That can be vital, as if you lose focus, or forget your plan, you will find that the next delivery rarely goes where you intended it to,

A cold towel on my head stops any danger of the steam rising during the tour of Sri Lanka in March 2012.

or else you end up bowling a short ball that the batsman is ready and waiting for.

There was a great example of just how vital it is to keep calm when we had a really tight game in the final twenty20 match against Pakistan in Abu Dhabi in February this year. We had to win the match to secure the series, and after we had scored just 129 for six, thanks largely to an impressive knock of 62 not out from Kevin Pietersen, the pressure was on at the end of the game as they closed in on their target.

If you lose focus, or forget your plan, you will find that the next delivery rarely goes where you intended it to.

In these situations, I always find I get more nervous when I'm watching, because when I'm actually involved in the action I'm so focused on my technique and my gameplan that I almost lose sight of the end result. In a tight game, as a captain you've got to keep an eye on the bigger picture, but as a bowler my main focus had to be on winning that one ball I was about to deliver. I recognise that if I win that ball, I can build the pressure on my opponent and move calmly on to the next delivery.

On this occasion, I brought myself back to bowl the penultimate over of the innings. Pakistan needed 17 runs in two overs, with seven wickets still in hand, and Umar Akmal and Misbah-ul-Haq were both well set. I kept my line wide of off stump, knowing that Akmal would want to work me through the leg side if he could, and varied my pace. After two dot balls, I'd created enough pressure that he heaved one high into the sky and it was taken at long-off. The batsmen crossed, and the next ball went for four after a slight misfield. It was a moment where I had to forget what had just happened and concentrate on winning the next ball. The end result of the fielding error was that we had lost that ball, but we were still winning the over. I made sure I kept to my plan, and the final two balls of the over did not yield any runs.

That left Jade Dernbach having to defend a target of 13 off the final over, which he was able to do, even though Pakistan could still have won it with a six off the last delivery. But throughout that over, I had to recognise that if the batsman scored a single it meant we had still won that ball, and our aim was then simply to win the next ball. If we thought in this straightforward way, by the end of the over we would surely win the match.

Twenty20 cricket is perhaps an extreme example, but I always try not to

Communication is vital if both bowlers are to work to the same plans. Here Andrew Strauss, Chris Tremlett and I make sure we are all working together.

look too far ahead. There's no point in my thinking: 'I want to win the Ashes next year by three-one.' Instead, it is important to focus on the next day and not worry about anything further in the future. The day before a match, all you can do is ensure you are ready to do the right things when the next day dawns. In those circumstances, I always think about winning the first over of the day, striking the first blow and stamping my authority on the game.

If I can do that at the beginning, I can build on my momentum and take things from there. This is why, conversely, I realise I can lose impetus if I'm not right from ball one. In the England team, we focus on getting it right in the first half-hour. Once that's out of the way, it's time to go again with the next period of the game, and to try to win that one as well.

In making this happen, one of England's biggest strengths as a team is our communication. We work together on our plan, and keep talking to each other about it. That's why not sending the bowler down to fine-leg after he's bowled an over gives him a chance to talk to his bowling partner. It also means we can share with each other what we are doing, so that our plan is maintained from both ends. If one of the bowlers has been getting the ball to move, we can chat to find out what it is they are doing and apply the same techniques. It really helps.

My routine when I come in to bat does not vary. The familiar habits make me feel immediately comfortable at the crease.

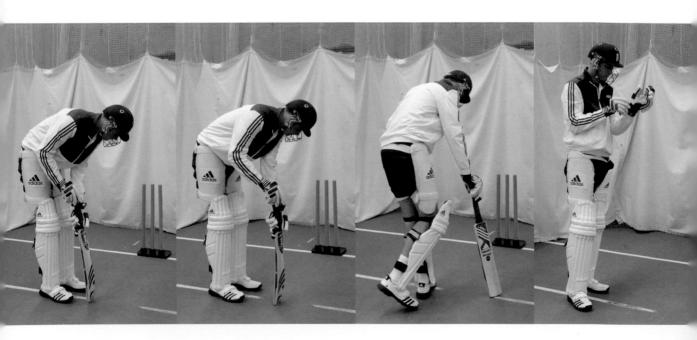

We work together to help us get the team off the field as quickly as possible (bowlers enjoy their rest-time in the pavilion!). In some sides that is not the case, and you can tell the bowlers are competing against each other to see who can take the most wickets, rather than wanting the team to do well. Much as I like taking wickets myself, as long as I am performing well and the side is running through the opposition, I really don't mind who picks up the most victims. I've learned to realise that if I'm not taking wickets, but bowling well, my time will come, so I mustn't worry about it. The fact that the selectors show faith in the players also helps in this, as it reduces the likelihood of unnecessary tension creeping in.

GETTING INTO THE HABIT

Ask most cricketers and they will tell you that they have certain habits or superstitions before they go out to play a match. Personally, I don't like

the word superstitions, as I think it makes it seem as though one is relying on certain things to be successful. I don't believe it should ever go that far. However, I do have various habits that help to make me feel comfortable in my surroundings.

For example, I like to scratch my mark three times when I go out to bat. I don't think it will be bad luck if I do it twice or four times instead.

Bowling at Cardiff in 2009, a Test match that saw the start of a strange superstition.

It's just a case of me marking my area. I think it's important to have your habits, but equally it's vital that it doesn't throw you off your stride if you can't do it. As I've mentioned, I like to have three practice balls to mid-off before I start a spell, but in one-day cricket that fielder might be back on the boundary, so I won't have anyone to bowl to, and also there just isn't time to go through that process. If bowling three balls were a superstition, this would be where it might get frightening, because what could I do to compensate in those circumstances? But, as it is just a habit it is fine, because I can simply bowl three balls in my mind instead.

I don't have any strange superstitions, such as carrying a teddy bear in my bag or anything like that. But cricketers, like all sportsmen, can be highly superstitious. For example, that occasion in 2009 when we batted out the final day at Cardiff to save the Test against Australia, Matt Prior had a tennis ball in the shower and he just bounced it all the time, because he couldn't bear to watch. Now he takes it with him all the time as he believes it will help bring the team luck.

The danger with a simple thing like this is when things start to go wrong. For example, I started to wear my Broad Appeal band at the beginning of the India series in 2011 and I did well and we won all the matches. During that series, I gave one to Matt and he also performed well against them. I didn't think too much about it, until I was playing in the garden with Matt's young son Jonathan, who is my godson. He was intrigued by it and asked me what it was, and then he accidentally broke it when he pulled at it. After that, we struggled against Pakistan in the UAE, so we started to blame the bands because mine had been broken. It was silly even to think like that.

While habits are important, because they set you up for what you're going to do and are part of your preparation, superstitions are to be avoided. There's a good story about Neil McKenzie, the Hampshire and South Africa batsman, who is known to be one of the more superstitious men on the circuit. One day, his team-mates decided to play a prank on him, and taped

> **I think it's important to have your habits, but equally it's vital that it doesn't throw you off your stride if you can't do it.**

> **The great advantage of being an opening bowler is that it is relatively easy to prepare myself mentally for action.**

his pads to the ceiling to see if they could get in his bubble and disrupt his concentration. It didn't work. He took them down and then went and scored a century. Nothing too remarkable in all that, perhaps. But it was what he did next that was truly surprising. Afterwards, he decided that he had to tape his pads to the ceiling every time before he went out to bat, in the apparent hope that doing so would bring him good luck!

Within the England team there are some superstitious players, too – Graeme Swann always wears the same pants and socks to bowl in. I must confess that I have succumbed to a similar thing, too. I was going through a bit of a rough time last summer and my mother bought me a pair of bright green socks before the Lord's Test match. She said they would be my lucky socks, and I've worn them to every match day since. I have washed them during that time, of course!

MIND ON THE JOB

The great advantage of being an opening bowler is that it is relatively easy to prepare myself mentally for action. If a match is going to start on the next day, I have to assume that we will field first, and get my mind set on bowling immediately. During the match, the captain will give me a few minutes' warning that he expects me to bowl soon. But none of this is true for me when I am a batsman. Once a wicket falls and I am due to go in, I have only a few seconds to make the final preparations before I am called into action. This requires a very different sort of mental preparation.

When I'm padded up and ready to go in to bat, I like to have conversation around me, but I don't want to get too involved in what is being said. Having a bit of a buzz going on around me helps me feel relaxed, as I find that silence just makes me more nervous. Fortunately, changing rooms are rarely quiet places anyway; there's lots of chat going on, but I keep a little bit away from it.

As I explained earlier, I try to keep an eye on the cricket outside, but I always watch the TV screen as well, because I can see a lot more of what the ball is doing on the television, which helps get me prepared for what I will have to deal with. We have the sound turned down all the time, as we don't want to be distracted by anything the commentators are saying on there. The reason for this is that sometimes what they are suggesting we ought to do may run counter to our own gameplan, or else their comments may have a negative impact on us. Either way, we need to keep our focus.

I will normally sit still in this position, unless after an hour or so there hasn't been a wicket, then I'll just move around a little so that I don't get too stiff. For me, this time is all about seeing what it's doing out there and picturing what I'm going to do. So if I can see that the ball is nipping about, I tell myself I must get forward and concentrate on leaving the ball well. If it's flat and the ball isn't doing much, I will get myself into a much more positive frame of mind, and start thinking about how I can take that bowler down if I have to go in and bat.

The important thing when you're preparing to go in is that you need to be switched on, but not as intensely alert as you would be if you were actually batting. This is because you might have to wait for a long time and you don't want to drain yourself of concentration before you even go out to bat.

When the wicket falls and it's my time to go in to bat, I stay sitting down for a moment, then put on my helmet and the rest of my gear. When I've done that, I get up, have three practice shots, and then head off to bat. At Trent Bridge, it's quite a long walk down the stairs to get out onto the pitch, so that gives me plenty of time to get my mind set on the task ahead. Lord's is another ground where it's a long walk down from the changing rooms, too, and the staircase looks the same all the way down. There's a famous story that David Steele used to tell of the time he was heading out to bat at Lord's – but he was so focused on what he was about to do that he ended up walking into the ladies' toilets instead, because he went down one flight of stairs too many.

And it's certainly the case that I need to be fully focused by the time I get out to the middle. The Aussies were famous for the welcome they'd give new

batsmen when they got out to the crease. I remember how, on some occasions, I'd walk out to bat and be taking middle and they'd be on at me immediately, slagging me off, insulting my family or whatever else they could think of to say, before I'd even faced a ball. What they were trying to do was to knock the batsman out of his routine and his comfort zone. So I knew that if I responded, even by asking 'What did you just say?', they would have succeeded in distracting me and upsetting my routine, and therefore made me much more vulnerable to getting out. Down the years that sort of verbal intimidation has helped them to get their wickets. As an incoming batsman, it's vital that you don't respond: the fielding side is already on a high, having just taken a wicket, so you don't want to give them any more encouragement if you possibly can.

I know that one of my roles is to give support to the batsman at the other end when I come in.

As well as preparing my mind to bat, I also have to think about what I can offer the side. I know that one of my roles is to give support to the batsman at the other end when I come in. I'm not sure this sort of thinking was so common for a Test number eight in the older days. But then things have changed. In my father's day, Bruce French was the wicket-keeper for England, and he would often bat at number eight, too. Yet he averaged just 18 in Tests, and those around him didn't have a much higher average either. Yet now we have Matt Prior who averages 42, Tim Bresnan on 40, me on 28, Swanny on 22. Part of the reason for this is the impact Graham Gooch has had on the lower order. It's not so much in terms of his technical input, but he has encouraged us all to think like a batsman and to have pride in what we do as a batsman. By ignoring our other roles as bowlers or as the wicket-keeper when we come in to bat and concentrating on being the best batsmen we can be, we have developed into an effective unit later on in the innings.

(*Left*) Celebrating my century at Lord's against Pakistan – a perfect example of where setting out to help my partner, Jonathan Trott, turned into something much more.

(*Overleaf*) Sitting under the Lord's honours board – I couldn't be more proud now that my name is on there, too.

KEEPING YOUR FOCUS

Going out to bat in the right state of mind can be difficult, as one can be distracted by what the fielders are saying, the form of the bowlers, or the state of the match. But it is still relatively easy compared to the challenges of maintaining your concentration over a long period, and not getting knocked out of your gameplan.

There was a famous occasion where Sachin Tendulkar had been nicking balls against Australia in 2003-04. He recognised that he had been getting out because he had been trying to drive at balls that weren't quite right for that shot, so he decided not to play the shot at all. If that shot was costing him his wicket, then he wouldn't play it. That decision made, he went out and scored 241 not out in Sydney, and there was about one drive in the whole innings. When you think about the mental application that took. He scored runs everywhere else, but when it was in the slot to play the drive, he just left it. That's the benchmark to aim for, and is just one reason why he has been such a great batsman for so many years. Of course, the rest of us can't be expected to take that massive leap forward, but I feel if I can just add a block on the wall each time I train, I can build up to get closer to it.

Sachin's example can be applied in a different way, too. One piece of advice I would give to anyone when they make a step up from one level to the next is this: you may be able to play every shot in the book, but some shots come more naturally than others, so when you move up stick to your strengths. If you know you pull well and clip off your legs well, stick to that – forget about the drive. Watch Alastair Cook – he keeps playing to his strengths during a Test match; he doesn't play the drive often. Similarly, when you have moved up, stick to your strengths and grow into your role. There is no point in trying to impress everyone with all that you can do, as the chances are that your over-confidence or eagerness will be your downfall. Instead, play within yourself and wait till you've got to 60 or so before showing off your range of shots. If it's a good enough approach for Sachin and Cook, it will work for you as well.

If keeping concentration going for long periods is one challenge, or playing within yourself, then arguably the biggest test comes when you're facing quick bowling and get hit by the ball. How do you respond to what's just happened? It's vital that the next ball you have to front up. I must admit that I love that sort of competitive stuff: to be honest, if you don't like that sort of thing, then you're probably not going to be cut out for Test cricket. But it's true at any level of the game: you have to show that you're not intimidated and that you're ready to take on the next challenge.

I can only imagine what it was like for England batsmen a generation or so ago when they were seeing their team-mates getting hit by the West Indies pacemen or Australia's Lillee and Thomson. In the 1970s, they had so little protection – not even helmets. We're lucky with the amount of protection we can wear these days, which has greatly reduced the risk of us getting seriously injured.

That thought brings me to another thing: any young bowler should understand that they have a responsibility to their side to protect themselves, which means wearing a chest guard. You're letting your team down if you get

A few verbal exchanges can sometimes help the bowler or the batsman knock his opponent out of his stride.

hit and get a rib broken, or can't bowl because the ball has injured you in some way. When I go in to bat I wear a very thin chest guard that goes beneath my Adidas underlayer, so that it is tight to my body and not easily visible. I don't feel that this means I'm being any less brave – I know that anyone can get hit at any time – but I am doing what I can to ensure I play a full role for my team.

However much I prepare to do the right thing and get myself mentally in the correct frame of mind, it still doesn't necessarily stop me from making a silly mistake or playing a rash shot. Sometimes I get lucky, and I'm dropped or the ball just misses my stumps, so I can have the chance to reset myself and continue. But on other occasions, I have to face the long walk back to the pavilion. Usually in England games, a cameraman will come out to record every

No matter how comprehensive the dismissal, it's important to move on in your own mind.

step of the journey back. This can make it feel as though the entire world is looking on and judging, but in reality they're not. Even those that are shaking their heads over the error they have just seen will soon move on to other things.

So the next point in the mental game is to learn that there's no point in beating yourself up about getting out. You don't need to listen to other people reminding you what a bad shot you've played, or whatever it is that you've done wrong – you know it yourself. Or you should do. And as Virender Sehwag once said: 'The sun will shine for another day.' (He wasn't speaking during the summer of 2012, of course!)

What is vital is how you bounce back from a setback. I respect the way that Rory McIlroy recovered from his collapse in the 2011 Masters and took his

next chance to win a major tournament. His courage in winning the US Open so soon after showed how he had learned from his previous experience, and was also able to shut out any doubts he might have had about holding on to his position at the top of the leaderboard at the start of the final day.

KEEPING YOUR MIND FRESH

When some people question the need for cricketers to have a break from the game, they tend to look only at the number of days we've actually spent on the field. But I hope this chapter has highlighted the fact that there is also some intensive mental preparation that needs to be done as well, and that this can be just as tiring. Therefore it is really important to rest and recharge myself, however reluctant I am to miss a game.

In actual fact, I find it a little bit easier to get away from cricket during the English summer than I do when I'm on tour. Although tours can be less intense, because I don't have the papers around me the whole time, on the other hand I know that I'm always 'on tour' when I'm playing a series abroad. When England are playing at home, I can get away from it totally when I'm not in action.

One way I've learned to get away from the cricket bubble is to play golf. I'm not a particularly good golfer (I play off about 18), but when I'm playing a round I have to focus on what I'm doing on the course. That takes my mind off worrying about any technical issues in my cricket game. Because golf requires so much concentration, it makes it a good way to escape. A round of golf therefore becomes a four-hour walk away from cricket. On the course, I must confess that I just try to hit the ball as far as I can. But I'm also lucky that I get to play at some really nice courses all over the country.

I learned about the benefits of this sort of escape at that time during the Ashes of 2009 when I went fishing with my dad. I think it's important, when you are getting a bit of stick and things aren't going right, that you get away. Paul Collingwood was quite instrumental in impressing that lesson on me. I was only just 23 at the time, and he showed his experience by telling me to go away for a few days. It was great advice and freshened me up, and I came back and got back-to-back five-fers.

That's something I still use to this day: if I feel I'm under the pump a little bit – I'll get away from it, even if it's just for a day or two days. It helps me to reset my mind. The intense scheduling we have now, with frequent back-to-back Tests, makes it hard to get away for a day's golf. But if I can, I know it gives me a chance to spend some time with my mates and talk about something that's not cricket. Unfortunately, during the English summer, it's amazing how if I'm not playing, I'm driving to my next venue or I'm training, so finding the time to recharge myself is not easy.

Having worked on getting my mind right and my body fit, it is now all about putting in a good performance. So in the next chapter we will look at those times when it all goes right: when everything comes together, whether it is with the bat, ball or in the field.

Watching Nottingham Forest is one way for me to get away from the mental stresses of cricket.

Sometimes if you're patient, your luck will change, and we are fortunate that in today's England set-up we are given that time.

Chapter 8

PERFORMING

If someone in the side does get injured their replacements will immediately be told what their role is.

However important it is to get the batting and bowling side of the game right, and to go into a game in the best frame of mind, with the ideal training behind you, there are other factors that can have a major impact on the final result on the field. One is to create the right atmosphere in the changing room. This is an aspect that is often overlooked, but it is easy to spot a side where everyone is playing for the team and their team-mates, and a side that is comprised of a group of individuals. When everyone is working together, this will be shown most obviously in the quality of their fielding, when the whole team has the opportunity to support each other in the task of dismissing the opposition.

CREATING A HAPPY CHANGING ROOM

A lot of the credit for England's recent success, and the strength we have in depth, has to be given to the environment created by the coach and captain, Andy Flower and Andrew Strauss. Sometimes, when come players into a side for the first time, they can feel a bit of an outsider. Indeed, that can even be the case for those who are returning to the side, too. It's not that way with England. When Monty Panesar came back to play for England during the series against Pakistan in the UAE, he had not been picked to play a Test for more than two years and might have felt a bit nervous or unsure about his role. But he was welcomed into the changing room and was given a role, so it was very clear to him what he was expected to do. Perhaps as a result of that support, Monty felt relaxed and so performed very well.

We know that if someone in the side does get injured, or if someone is rested, their replacements will immediately be told what their role is and how they're expected to carry it out. That's why when, for example, Jonathan Trott came into the side in 2009, he made a century on debut in an Ashes Test. These sorts of things aren't coincidence; he did well because he was made to feel at home.

The other part of creating a happy changing room is not just about making newcomers feel happy, but recognising when the regular players also need support. For a top batsman, this can be done by simply reminding him that his time will come. For example, Alastair Cook had had a tough period in the summer of 2010, scoring just 106 runs in eight Test knocks up to the second

In recent times, England have been very good at helping to create the right atmosphere for all the players involved.

Like other great coaches and managers, Flower does create something of a fear factor around himself.

I think both of us would want to recognise the support we got from all those around us in the England set-up, including Strauss and Flower. We will look more closely at the role of the captain in the next chapter, but the other key figure in England's recent successes has been Flower. Like other great coaches and managers, he does create something of a fear factor around himself. This is fine: look at someone such as Sir Alex Ferguson, the manager of Manchester United. He doesn't ever set out to be a player's friend, and he's someone who does not seem to be easily pleased or satisfied – he always wants to get more out of his players. Flower is similar. He will build up a player and boost their confidence if they need it, but he is not afraid to give them a bollocking, too. At times, all players need to be reassured or pushed forward. But where Flower is good is that he understands when people need the stick or the carrot, and he also believes in giving us the chance to go with our instincts.

A good example of this came on the first day of the Test against India at Trent Bridge in 2011. The first two sessions had been dominated by the Indian bowlers, and so I found myself having to go out to bat just before tea when we were 117 for seven. It soon got worse, when Ian Bell nicked one the last ball before the break to make us 124 for eight.

I went in for tea knowing that it was going to be me and Graeme Swann walking out afterwards, and that in theory it might take two more balls to finish us off. So I thought there didn't seem to be any point in us trying to block out, when the ball was swinging about so much, in the hope that we could nudge and nurdle our way up to 150 or so. Instead, it struck me that if I just planted my foot down the pitch and swung my bat, I might get lucky. There weren't many fielders who were going to catch it out in the field, as they had four slips and a gully.

I found Flower walking around in his office, and I asked him about taking that approach. He agreed and simply said: 'I think it's your best option.' Swanny and I put

On the counterattack, my knock against India at Trent Bridge in 2011 may not have won any style points, but it helped change the momentum of the game.

on 73 together, and it didn't take us long. I have to admit it wasn't the most beautiful batting – there were some ugly shots – but even that got under the Indians' skin.

I remember hitting Sreesanth for four with an inside edge that went in completely the wrong direction from where it was meant to go, and he let rip with a barrage of abuse at me because he was feeling so frustrated. Suddenly he was trying every sort of variation to get me out, even though it was still a seaming wicket that was giving the bowlers plenty of help. I reckon that if he'd just kept on doing what he had been doing, he'd most likely have got me out. I know as a bowler it is hard not to change things, but as a batsman when you see that happening, that's when you know you've got on top of them.

There's a lot that goes on out in the middle when I'm batting in a Test match. When I'm in a partnership like that one, we might end up talking about where we're going for dinner that evening. Contrastingly, we might be geeing each other up and telling one another to keep our intensity high, for example: 'This is a crucial part of the Ashes series, let's dig in.' Sometimes I've even ended up getting in a competition with my partner to see who can score the most runs. It all depends on the state of the game. But whatever the circumstances, I always try to have a smile on my face when I'm batting, to express myself and to enjoy it. Even if I am smiling, that doesn't mean I don't recognise that there are also times when I have to be a 'run-getter', as Graham Gooch describes it, and dig in.

While working together as a batting partnership is one aspect of teamwork, it is in the field that good teamwork can become most important, as it is there that the whole team is together in action.

WORKING IN THE FIELD

In the old days, fielders tended to have a long walk in as the bowler was running up – it wasn't especially dynamic, but everyone knew that this was what one had to do, so they did it. In some cases, one could sense that fielders were almost going through the motions. Now we've changed that approach:

we tend to wait until the bowler has almost reached the umpire before starting to walk in. But when we start, we move with much greater intensity. It's a short and dynamic effort, so that we really are ready for action.

CATCHING

When catching the ball, the key is to get your hands and your eyes close together, so that you can watch the ball right into your hands. But while doing that, you also have to ensure you don't get too cramped up.

I prefer the Australian way of catching under the high ball, where you hold your hands up with fingers pointing up, whereas the English way is usually to take the catch lower down. The advantage of the Aussie way of doing things is that if you get it wrong, you may get another chance before the ball reaches the ground; with the English way, there's almost no hope of catching the rebound.

There are a few other important things you can do to give yourself the best chance of taking a catch: put the legwork in to get right underneath the ball,

When catching, it is important to keep your hands and eyes close together, and to have a steady base.

so you can catch with a strong base – you don't want to be stretching or on the move if you can avoid it. The next thing to achieve is to keep your head as still as possible, even if only at the last moment before the ball arrives. Finally, make sure your hands, if you are holding them high, don't interrupt your view of the ball.

On the whole these methods seem to have worked for me, as I'm pleased to say that I haven't missed too many in my career. I do remember one I dropped, in Bangladesh in a one-day match, but in my defence I started to have a back spasm as the ball came towards me and I couldn't move, so in the end it just hit me as I could do nothing about it.

GROUND FIELDING

When attacking the ball in the field, it is best to come at it from as low a position as possible. Unfortunately, that's slightly harder for me at my height, but it is important to make that effort. The next stage is to get into the throwing position as quickly as possible: my front foot points in the direction I want to throw, while my back foot gives me the power to launch it as hard as I can. My left arm and feet all point in the same direction as I throw.

If the ball comes to me on my 'wrong' side (ie to my left hand), rather than try to stop it with my weaker hand I aim to get both hands to it, reversing

Note how I come in low to pick up the ball, and when throwing my feet point in the direction I'm aiming.

my right hand to help with the pick-up. When doing this, I make sure my foot is planted as close to the ball as possible, then I can turn round and get my body weight going back to the stumps when I throw it in. In this way, my back foot drives me forward into the throw. Of course, some people may feel more comfortable picking up the ball with their wrong hand, but I feel this way helps me to get into position more quickly to let go of the ball.

In the batting sections, we looked at the way that many players will target those who field at mid-off or mid-on for a quick single. Because of this, it can also be one of the better positions to try to get a run-out. If I'm trying to run someone out, the principles involved remain similar to fielding the ball at other times: I aim to get my foot close to the ball and try to release the ball at the stumps quickly, within one stride. I attack the ball with a low body position.

However, don't forget that fielding in this position can also create problems that don't arise elsewhere, because at mid-off and mid-on the ball can bobble as it comes across the bowlers' footmarks. Therefore, it is even more important that I keep my eye on it all the way into

Picking the ball up with one hand reversed isn't easy, but it means I can throw in much more quickly when I've picked it up.

When trying to run someone out, a quick release is vital – but make sure you have gathered the ball safely first before thinking about the throw.

my hands. But the key piece of advice when trying to run someone out is this: don't think about the run-out until you have got the ball in your hands. It's a two-stage process, so focus on one stage at a time. Gather the ball safely in your hands, and only then think about the quick release to shy at the stumps.

There's also been plenty of recent debate about where a bowler should stand at the stumps when the ball is being thrown in from the outfield. The old-school approach was to stand behind the stumps, so if the ball has a chance to hit the stumps it can do so. Inevitably, this will be the quickest way to get someone out. If it misses, you can take it and whip the bails off. The new method is to get your foot as close as possible to the stumps, but to stand in front of them, so you know where they are. Then when the ball comes in you can take off the bails with your elbow – you don't have to move your hands with the ball in them to break the stumps. In a tight run-out situation, this method can make all the difference.

Standing in front of the stumps with my foot next to them ensures I can take the bails off as quickly as possible.

This sort of thinking and analysis, making small adjustments where necessary, is a continual process in the England team. We are always looking for new ways to give ourselves the slightest advantage, and that is one of the key roles that any captain needs to bring to his game when it comes to getting the tactics right.

(*Left*) Diving to make my ground safely after a quick single – it's surprising how many runs can be picked up if you go for it.

Whether or not you've been given the role, I think any cricketer should always be thinking as if he were the captain.

Chapter 9

TACTICAL

Even if you're not a bowler thinking about your next spell, it is still possible to play a captain's role.

In May 2011, I was appointed captain of England's twenty20 side – a very proud moment in my career to date. Since that time, the role of England captain has been split three ways: Andrew Strauss is in charge of the Test side, Alastair Cook runs the 50-over team, and then there's me as skipper in the shortest format. I've always been interested in the tactical side of the game, and this relatively new role has given me a great opportunity to develop that aspect of my understanding of cricket.

ON CAPTAINCY

I'd like to think that when I took on the job, it wasn't a complete leap into the unknown. Whenever I've stepped onto a cricket pitch, I've always had the mindset of a captain. Whether or not you've been given the role, I think any cricketer should always be thinking as if he were the captain. By this, I don't mean that everyone in the side should be sharing every opinion they have with the captain, but certainly I believe that every bowler should be watching how the batsmen are playing. They should be thinking about what lines they ought to be bowling, and whether a fielder should be moved slightly to protect a shot that the batsman seems to enjoy playing. And, even if you're not a bowler thinking about your next spell, it is still possible to play a captain's role: for example, if you notice that a bowler needs a bit of lift then give him some encouragement; or if you see that things are going a little flat, try to gee up the rest of the side in the field.

I've always thought in this way so, since I came into the role in 2011, I've been pleased to be able to give full expression to the tactical side. I enjoy thinking about the game, and being captain gives me plenty of scope to do that. Unsurprisingly, I've been a massive cricket fan since I was a boy, and even when I'm watching a game on television, I will find myself getting involved in

Alastair Cook, Andrew Strauss and I pose for the cameras at Lord's in May 2011 when England decided to have three captains for the three formats of the game.

Twenty20 captaincy is extremely intense, because each ball is vital, especially as the innings progresses.

across his stumps to try to work me to leg, and this made it harder for him to do.

One thing I have found, which might surprise people who see the game as being very simple, is that twenty20 captaincy is extremely intense, because each ball is vital, especially as the innings progresses. But while every ball is highly significant, I am also aware as a captain that I need the bowler to be comfortable with what we're trying to do and to be as relaxed as possible. He's the one who has to deliver the ball, so he has to know the field he wants and be happy with it. The last thing I want is a bowler who tells me he doesn't mind what field I set. I want him to say: 'I'm going to bowl a leg-stump yorker, so we can bring third man up into the ring and have someone back on the leg side in case it gets hit there.' Because of this, on the whole, I don't intervene too much in setting the field; it's important to give the bowler responsibility.

I can still give some advice, of course. Particularly in twenty20 cricket, a batsman will often move around the crease as the bowler is about to deliver the ball. In this situation, I would give different advice according the circumstances. If the batsman is new to the crease, it's really hard for him to do this effectively, so I'd suggest still aiming at the stumps as he's quite likely to miss the ball.

If a batsman is more established and he moves to the leg side, you know he wants width, so fire it in at his boots; whereas if he moves to the off, it's clear he's looking to flick the ball to leg, so follow them with the line you bowl. For a bowler in this situation where a batsman is trying to disrupt him, it is important to change the line and nothing else, don't also change the type of ball you were planning to bowl, for example suddenly deciding to bowl a slower one. If you overreact to the batsman, you may just end up bowling wides or getting it all wrong. Then the batsman has won: they've tried to put you off and they have succeeded. So my advice in these circumstances is to keep calm and don't change your plan, just change the line.

In any format of cricket, the captain and the bowler need to work together. In the Test side, I can't remember an occasion when Straussy has changed my field without talking it through with me, and the same would be true of Jimmy, Swanny or any of the other bowlers. At the top level, the guys who will be successful are those who can make their own decisions. Sometimes, of course, the bowler will have a plan, and the captain may suggest they try something else, and you then agree a new strategy. That's part of a captain's role. And both a captain and a bowler have to adapt their strategy if circumstances dictate that they need to. For example, if a bowler's yorker isn't coming out quite right in one game, it would make no sense to keep going with a plan that involves bowling lots of yorkers – he has to try something else instead.

As a twenty20 captain, my role when England are batting is relatively limited. My main job is to ensure my batsmen have the freedom to play their natural game while still paying attention to their responsibilities to their team-mates. If someone was to say to me that they felt they could hit a certain bowler over long-off, I would say that they should play the shot, but don't do it recklessly. The only other thing I have to bear in mind is to be adaptable; for example, it might make sense to change the batting order. If I were considering doing this, it is something I might discuss with Andy Flower before we altered our plans.

This sort of flexibility is relatively unusual in Test cricket, while in twenty20 cricket you sometimes have to go more with your gut feeling, because you can't plan it in quite the same way. In Tests, if a batsman is struggling to find their touch, it makes sense to persist with him and allow him the time to come through the tough spell, even if it means him gritting out a slow, ugly fifty. In a 20-over series, it might make sense to change things around, as you can't be sure beforehand who will be getting it bang on. There's no time for a batsman to ease his way back into form.

With the bowling attack, I think it's important to save death bowlers for the end, but up until then it makes sense to go with your instinct as to who will have the best chance to get a particular batsman out. By contrast, in Test matches, it is possible to plan it a bit more: for the first hour at least, the seamers are going to bowl, and then it might be worth giving the spinner a go, especially if the batsmen seem to be getting settled.

Despite this need for flexibility, I would also add that the biggest part of my job as captain is ensuring that players know their roles in the side. For example, when we won the World Cup in 2010, all the bowlers knew when they were going to bowl their overs. So I knew I could come on for the fourth and sixth overs, and then come back to bowl the 15th and 17th overs – I did it all tournament. Perhaps because we all knew exactly what was expected of us, we were all nailing it.

Obviously, by giving everyone clear roles, we could create a situation when we might become too predictable, so we have to look at the conditions and the batsmen concerned. We might, for example, open with a spinner, if it was a turning wicket, just to change things. It's about striking the right balance between having a clear strategy in which everyone knows their role, yet still being adaptable.

A good example of this came in Abu Dhabi earlier in 2012. I decided to bowl Steven Finn for three overs at the start, because we'd made a relatively low score, so there was no point leaving him with his normal two to bowl at the end of the innings, in case we never got that far. It made more sense to have our main strike bowler having a longer spell at the beginning to try to pick up more wickets and put the pressure on Pakistan. The more the game went on, when it seemed like it would go the whole distance, the more I realised that I would need to hold back myself and Jade Dernbach, so we could bowl at the death. Otherwise, we might have bowled earlier on. Happily, it seemed to work on that occasion, as we ended up winning the game. As a captain, that was a result that brought me a great deal of satisfaction, as the decisions I took worked out in our favour.

I'm also helped by having some good people around me that I can talk things through with: Straussy's one of the best captains ever, and then there's Andy Flower, and I'm also close to Michael Vaughan, another very successful England captain. I find that the more I talk to them and others whose opinions and knowledge I respect, the more I get to know things, and so the more comfortable I feel in my decision-making. This transmits itself to the players, who will happily support me to carry out my plans. That's why I was so pleased when we won the series in Abu Dhabi in such a pressurised situation. Jade must have got so much confidence from bowling as well as he did then, so

Steven Finn, who has evolved into one of my main strike bowlers in the twenty20 side, watches on during an England practice session.

CAPTAINS AND MENTORS

In my role as captain, I feel that I have been very lucky in the people I've been able to learn from – not just other captains I've played under, but also senior players who have been influential figures in my career. One of the most important attributes I have picked up from Strauss is that he always stays very calm, and furthermore he remains logical about what it is that we need to do in any given situation. His emotions are always very even, so if we have a bad session in the field he won't lay into us all, he'll just say things calmly like: 'We didn't have a good session just then, but looking forward to the next session let's try and bang some maidens together in the first half, let's lift our energy levels in the field and create pressure. Let's go!'

I've recognised that his approach is a positive way of going about things, rather than yelling at people. Bowlers are usually seen as being more emotional or fiery than batsmen, and so to see how being calm can help produce results was especially important for me. I've come to recognise that the way a captain looks and behaves has a real impact; if he's frantic, then that can lead to your team being frantic as well, and so there is a danger that all the plans go out the window.

I haven't played under too many captains who rant and rave, but in all honesty what do you get out of it? The way a team improves is by having clear points made – we need to do this and that – and then going out and doing it. A captain who tears into someone, telling a bowler that he can't seem to bowl straight that day, doesn't help in any way. If there's a problem, a captain's focus is simple. He just needs to ask himself: 'How am I going to improve it?' Letting his emotions run away with him, because he is frustrated that his plans haven't been well executed, achieves nothing.

Being captain of England has one great advantage, of course, in addition to the fact that you know you are playing alongside the best cricketers in the country. And that is the fact that you are playing with people who have real passion for the England team. This aspect is a strong part of our make-up: we know we are representing our country, and that gives us an enormous lift.

Some might cynically wonder about the likes of Jonathan Trott, who was born and raised in South Africa, on that issue. But he has a British passport and has made this country his home since 2002. So he is just as passionate as the rest of us to do well for his country and for his team-mates. Some show it differently, of course. But watch what happens when we take a wicket in the Ashes or at a vital time: everyone goes wild. That shows that everyone's in it together. We know it takes a lot of hard work to get a wicket, so when we do we want to celebrate.

After all the hard work, it's time to celebrate.

My first England captain was Vaughan, and he was calm like Strauss, but he probably tinkered about with the field more than Strauss does. He was always looking for a new fielding position, making a change and getting involved. But it's possible that some of that may just be that when I was playing for him, I was new in the set-up and so I needed more help, while with Strauss I'm more established. I thoroughly enjoyed Vaughan's approach: he was positive and I felt I had his support. That's one reason why I enjoy captaining in twenty20 cricket, because I can ask positive things: what are we going to do to make this ball a dot ball? In any format of cricket, it is vital to take things forward and focus on what can be done, rather than dwelling on the last ball that has just gone to the boundary.

As I've mentioned, as captain I've found that my focus on my own game has taken more of a back seat. This has meant that I've become more philosophical when things don't go right. If someone edges me for four, I recognise that there wasn't a lot I could have done to stop that happening, so let's just move it forward. If that had happened earlier in my career, I'd have been much more frustrated and cross, even though deep down I would have known that the batsman had been lucky, and that was all.

Fortunately, I remember what I was like in my early days, and I also recall the things that helped me to settle into my role. In my first season at Leicestershire, West Indies bowler Ottis Gibson was a big help to me. He would always let me have the wind behind me when it came to a choice of ends. It sounds a tiny thing, but as a young lad running in, it really did help. I felt I was being given the best chance to shine, so I felt really positive. On my England twenty20 debut, Darren Gough did the same thing – I remember there was a howling wind at Bristol, and he just said: 'It's all yours.' It was awesome and a great way of making me feel that I belonged.

In my batting, I didn't really have the same sort of mentor at Leicestershire as I did with Ottis when it came to bowling. Perhaps this was because I was seen as primarily a bowler, and there wasn't the same emphasis on building me up as a batsman. James Whitaker was the batting coach, and Ottis Gibson

Celebrating after Leicestershire won the Twenty20 Cup in 2006 – my first taste of county silverware.

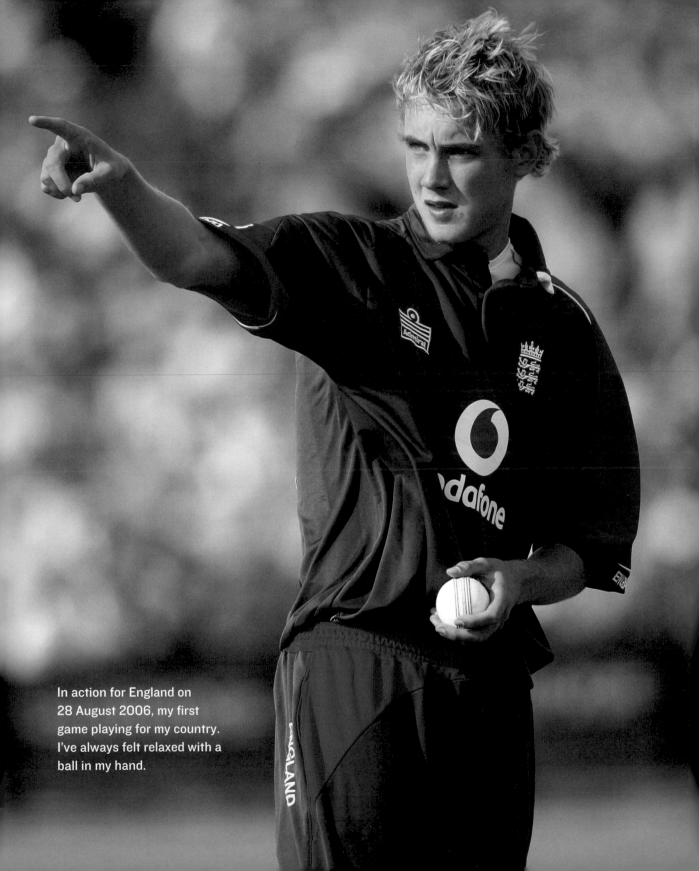

In action for England on
28 August 2006, my first
game playing for my country.
I've always felt relaxed with a
ball in my hand.

was also influential, while the main batsmen in the side were H.D.Ackermann, Darren Maddy and Paul Nixon. Nicko was a really good, positive character to play with, and he had a major impact in the changing room. I would say that he and Ottis were my biggest influences during my Leicestershire days.

Even though these people helped me, I still needed to work things out for myself. For example, at schoolboy level and in the second XI I'd rarely faced a bouncer, but suddenly I was finding that I was having to face lots of them. My mum has a picture of me evading a bouncer that someone bowled at me in a game against Worcestershire in June 2005. It was my third first-class match, and you can see how I've jerked my head back to avoid it. It was a welcome to serious cricket. I had to learn how to cope with that sort of delivery very quickly, or else I would have found that the message got round the circuit that I was afraid of bouncers – a surefire way to finding myself facing many more.

I must admit I found it a baptism of fire coming into county cricket. Almost at once, I had to face Andy Caddick at Taunton. Beforehand, I'd never faced anyone with any genuine pace, and he had a real aura about him and a presence. The first ball he bowled at me whizzed past my nose. I remember thinking: 'That was rapid.' Having come from schoolboy cricket, where I opened the batting, I now found myself down the order and realised what a lot of work I had to do if I was going to survive at this level. It took me a year to make my first half-century (in my 25th innings). Essentially I wasn't as well prepared for the batting side of the professional game as I was for the bowling side. I was really relaxed about the bowling, because I knew that if I pitched it up at the stumps and got it to move away, I had a chance. Bowl a good ball and you can get anyone out.

Unfortunately, at first-class level I got to face a fair few, too, which meant I got out more easily than I would have liked. As I mentioned earlier on, I had to learn not to chase after the ball and to build into my innings. Eventually, I started making more runs and my confidence grew as I began to realise that I could cope at this level. I also began to learn about the importance of working together in partnerships.

Essentially I wasn't as well prepared for the batting side of the professional game as I was for the bowling side.

PARTNERS

One of the things that I enjoy about my role batting for England is that I'll almost always come in to bat with someone who averages over 40 at the other end. My primary responsibility is to give him a chance to go and get runs, so I have to stay with him. There's no point in me throwing it away, because I'm not only losing my wicket, but also preventing someone else from making a much bigger score if I stick around with him. We sometimes use the word 'fearless' about the approach we want to take, but I don't think that's quite the right one. We all have a responsibility to our team-mates and to our country. It's about how we can take the next positive move, and so much of that depends on who we are batting with.

Unlike an opening bat, I have to get used to batting with different sorts of personalities. When Graeme Swann and I are batting together, we often just have a laugh. I remember the Ashes Test at Headingley in 2009, when I hit Stuart Clark for three fours in an over and was trying to smash every ball. Afterwards, Swanny came down to talk to me at the end of the over and said: 'If you think that was good, watch this!' Between us we put on about 40 in three overs – we just went wild. That was all about us both trying to outdo each other, and the situation of the game allowed us to play like that.

Jonathan Trott is at the other end of the scale. Trotty takes his time going through his routine, even between overs while the fielders are moving to position, so eventually I'll get down to have a word with him and all he says is: 'Five more.' He works in batches of five runs, so if we've put on 112 together, at the end of the over he'll just mention the next target – 115 – and that's it. He's all about accumulation, pure and simple, and it is an approach that has brought him a huge amount of success for England.

Matt Prior is different again. Matty and I will talk about the positive options we can see we could take against the bowlers we are facing, because we both play that way. Our conversation is about how we can take down a bowler, even if he's been bowling well at us, and those who have already batted. Despite this, we'll still look for any weaknesses and target them. At Lord's this year against the West Indies, he got a century and I got 75 not out – but what was really important was that we did it in about 25 overs. That's part and parcel of being in a team – working with different batsmen and their differing approaches for the maximum results.

Indeed, it's one of the more interesting parts of batting where I do in the order. A lot of what I have to do is to judge scenarios and, often, to try to change the momentum of things – that's why it's exciting, because every innings is so different. There's a time when I have to throw the wood at it, but also a time when I need to dig in.

It's fair to say that I'm not usually one to play a slow, gritty innings, but that's because I naturally score fast. One reason for this is that I'm tall and can

Standing with Matt Prior, one of my more regular batting partners – together we always look for the attacking option.

To me, it's not just about how people play their particular sport, it is also about how they conduct themselves.

score off balls that other shorter batsmen might struggle to reach. Also as a lower-order batsman, opponents are quick to put fielders out, as they assume that I won't play the cautious percentages in the way of a top-order batsman. This is fine, as it gives me the option of scoring easy singles. I also now have the advantage of knowing that I can bat for 300 balls, as I did against Pakistan, and that knowledge gives me more confidence that I can bat for a long spell if needed.

I know I can't expect an easy ride when I come out to bat. In the old days, there was the so-called 'bowlers' union', where fast bowlers might take it a little bit easier on the fellow bowlers in the knowledge that if they tried to rough them up, then they would get a dose of their own medicine back at them. This no longer applies. One of our philosophies as an England bowling attack is to try to nail the tail, because we're not only taking their wickets, but we might make it harder for them to bowl against us if they take a blow on their ribs. This means they will be less capable of putting our batsmen under pressure. The only time the bowlers' union exists nowadays is when we're bowling at our team-mates in the nets. I must admit, I've not always been as good as I would like to be at finishing off the tail, and know I have to work on this aspect of my game. When I watch someone like Dale Steyn of South Africa in action, I'm impressed at the way he can destroy the tail.

He's one of the bowlers in the world game today that I most admire, but there have been others in the past who have helped inspire me, as well as figures from other sports. But, to me, it's not just about how people play their particular sport, it is also about how they conduct themselves, and what I can learn from them in a world that is now – thanks to camera phones and Twitter, and all the rest of it – so instantly accessible to everyone. Life in the public eye has changed out of all recognition of late, and we are all trying to come to terms with what this means.

One of my targets is to get better at nailing the tail.

It isn't easy to get used to being in the public eye – and there are no training manuals to tell you what to do.

Chapter 10

LIFESTYLE

After England won the Ashes in 2009, the level of attention I received increased hugely.

THE PUBLIC EYE

Any sportsperson these days who has had some success, or who is seen in action regularly on television, will soon find that they are a subject of great public curiosity. It isn't easy to get used to this – and there are no training manuals to tell you what to do, after all; so, like everyone else, I have had to find my own way through the potential pitfalls while still remaining true to myself and my personality.

After England won the Ashes in 2009, the level of attention I received increased hugely – not just for me, but for everyone in the side. Some of the players had been through it all in 2005, and they had some words of advice, but it was all new to me. So it was that I was asked to do *The Jonathan Ross Show* on BBC1 at the beginning of September, just after the Test series had concluded.

It was the first such interview I'd ever done, and it was really quite hard, especially as I'd not had a chance to meet him before, having gone to the studio straight from a team meeting, and so I feared the worst might happen. I'd spoken to Fred Flintoff beforehand, as I knew he'd been on the show himself, and he advised me not to do it, because he'd felt that Jonathan Ross had focused more than he would have liked on his drinking escapades. But I reckoned that was unlikely to happen with me, as I've never been caught up in any big stories on that front.

In fact, Jonathan Ross was great with me, and because I arrived late I didn't really have time to get nervous. Instead, I spent an hour in the green room with Ricky Gervais, which was brilliant. As the show came to a close, I ended up bowling at them on the set of the show; they all had their England shirts on, and Ricky Gervais was given a tiny little box to protect himself.

While I was nervous about appearing on TV to be interviewed, it probably wasn't the most nervous I've been when it comes to media work I've undertaken. I have also had some unexpected and unusual requests from magazines to do shoots. Back in 2008, *Cosmopolitan* asked me, Jimmy Anderson and Alastair Cook to pose naked for them. It was for the Everyman charity, which raises awareness about male cancer, and so that helped make it easier as it was for a good cause, but we had only a cricket bat to cover ourselves.

That was probably the most 'out there' thing I have done. Jimmy, for example, has done the front cover of *Attitude* magazine, but perhaps that's an easier decision to make when you're married with two kids. I feel it is important to be careful where I place myself – I'm not a big lads' mag fan, so I've tended to steer clear of that end of the market.

Perhaps because of shoots such as the one for *Cosmopolitan*, I got a bit of a reputation as being one of the pin-up boys of the England team. I find it quite funny how some people can perceive me in that way, but of course the lads immediately jumped on the bandwagon, too. They have given me some stick for taking a lot of time over my appearance, but that's so far away from how I am. In truth, I'll take about five minutes to get changed. But, despite this, Graeme Swann still does a long and involved impression of me getting ready in front of the mirror. Believe me, there are plenty of others in the England side who take much longer to get dressed than I do!

Having said all of that, I do have one weakness when it comes to clothes. I like to dress up in a smart suit if I'm doing a photo shoot, as it's nice to show a different side of myself, rather than always being photographed in sportswear. For those who have to wear suits all the time for work, I can understand that they wouldn't see the appeal of doing that, but for me it's a big change from my usual stuff. Whenever I put on my England suit, it is a special occasion, which is one reason why I associate wearing suits with

looking smart and with significant moments. Given my size, suits have to be tailored for me, which again helps to make wearing one seem just that bit more special.

While television and the press are traditional parts of media life, the last few years have seen the rise of Twitter. Several of the England side are on it – I didn't start until the end of 2010, but Jimmy and Swanny led the way in the team. They decided to have a competition to see who could get the most followers in a month, and it went from there. Unfortunately, at first they didn't understand how to turn off their notifications (the email message you get that tells you someone has become one of your followers), so they might come off the pitch after a day's play and find that they had thousands of emails clogging up their inbox notifying them about the latest individuals who had joined in.

Twitter is quite an interesting concept; I believe that it has done us as a team some favours, because those who follow us can see a bit of banter between the players and get new insights into our lives. That said, we have to recognise how to use it, and more importantly how not to use it: it can be quite disturbing to go on there during a Test match and find that people are slagging you off for something you've done in the course of the game.

I think it's important to keep a good public profile in what I send out on Twitter – I'm amazed that the FA lets people such as Joey Barton say some of the things he does. The ECB are quite clever in the way they respond to anything we post where they feel we might have stepped out of line. They don't tell us that we've let ourselves down, instead they say that we're damaging the brand of cricket. They have helped to create a sense of group responsibility among us all. If we're told we'll all be banned from using it if one of us steps out of line again, then we tend to be much better at policing ourselves.

It's always important to me to look my best when the camera lens is pointed in my direction.

For me, one of the biggest plus points of being in the public eye is that it enables me to give support to things that I care about.

I always make a rule of never swearing on Twitter, and I don't understand how those in the public eye, especially sportspeople, can swear in public, because someone is always going to come down on us, saying it is inappropriate behaviour. Actors and musicians can get away with a lot more, as the rest of the media seem to feel they don't need to be seen as role models to quite the same extent as those who play sport for a living. In the England team, our guideline is: if we wouldn't say it in a press conference, then don't say it on Twitter. I'm not going to swear in front of 200 press, so why would I swear on Twitter?

For all that life in the public eye can have some drawbacks – having a private life becomes more difficult, and I have to maintain a level of good behaviour, even if I'm out with some mates or if someone tries to hassle me – it also has its definite benefits. For me, one of the biggest plus points is that it enables me to give support to things that I care about.

Perhaps the most important of these activities is The Broad Appeal, a charity that I lead with my father and sister Gemma. We set it up after my step-mother Miche fell victim to Motor Neurone Disease. I do six or seven days a year for the charity, trying to raise money to help people with the disease. When Miche was diagnosed with the illness in 2009, we found that when we went online, it was full of horrible stories of what to expect. The accounts seemed to focus on all the worst cases, and there was little positive information about what one can do to help; it was all very depressing.

Part of the charity's aim, therefore, is to help people to avoid having that reaction. In Miche's case, while she was battling against the illness, she tried to live as normal a life as possible for as long as she could, which showed that some positives were possible. It remains true that there is no cure for the disease, but that doesn't mean that nothing can be done. While the case studies online don't give much hope, there is research going on at the moment that might help find a cure, even if it will take some time. Last year The Broad Appeal raised some £140,000, which is a useful sum, and I hope we will continue to raise much more over the years to come.

Life in the public eye also gives me some wonderful opportunities to enjoy myself, too. I have a terrific group of sponsors and I am very fortunate because a lot of the work I do with them is great fun and they get me away from what I would do in everyday life. My Red Bull appearances are very different – they might take me to go and see a Grand Prix race or just as easily I will be asked to judge who has built the best boat to go down the Red Bull Rapids at the National Watersports Centre in Nottingham. With Jaguar, our Team England sponsor, I get to thrash a car around a race track.

Sometimes, a sponsor's day just gives me an excellent opportunity to take me back to what cricket is all about: with Adidas, for example, I went to coach a group of about 15 kids up to the age of 14 at Lord's. I must admit it made

I wear my Broad Appeal band to help raise the profile of this charity, which works to help those with Motor Neurone Disease.

me feel great to see the happiness on their faces as they charged around. They were full of questions, asking me about what it feels like to walk out at Lord's, or where I sit in the changing room, or what it's like to be on the honours board, and how many times I bowl in practice.

I told them what it felt like to go into an England changing room at the age of 20 and see my heroes, players such as Marcus Trescothick, in there. It was an awesome feeling. Even now, I'm certainly not one of those guys who can walk into a changing room and believe that I own the place, so I had to admit to them that it took a while to get used to it all. That's why, when we get new guys in the England changing room now, I believe it's important to remember what it was like for me and make them feel welcome. I think we're really good at that now, but in those days it was hard for newcomers, especially as the old Ashes 2005 side was beginning to break up as we began to move towards the squad we have now.

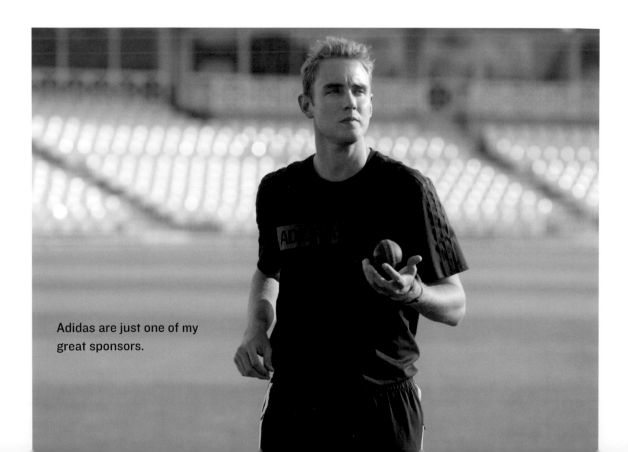

Adidas are just one of my great sponsors.

It's nice to do these things, because they give me new opportunities. But I also have to be very strict with myself about what I take on. That's where I'm fortunate in having Neil Fairbrother as my manager. He fully understands that performing on the field is everything, and that nothing must be allowed to distract me from being able to do my best as a cricketer. I recognise that sponsors are interested in me largely because I play for England. If my form suffered, and I lost my place, I am sure that I would become less interesting to the sponsors. I know it would be easy to fill my diary with sponsors' events on top of all the cricket work I do, but I also need to have breaks. Part of being a sportsman is learning how to deal with those things well.

Despite the fun we had, and the enormous privilege of playing for my country, I was still slightly awe-struck when I first joined the England set-up.

> **You have to put in the work for your sport. Furthermore, you have to make sure you still have your down time.**

I remember when I started with England in 2006, there were so many offers to do things that I thought I'd try to do it all. I was so excited by being given so many great opportunities. But then I realised: I was there to bat and bowl, not to go off on some jolly. I had to focus on my job. There are some sportspeople who get the balance wrong between work and the extra-curricular opportunities. But I believe that for those who do get it wrong, it will always show up. You have to put in the work for your sport. Furthermore, you have to make sure you still have your down time.

There are some who forget that a Test match isn't just for five days, which is why getting that down time can be hard. Our schedule, ahead of a Test starting on Thursday, will usually go something like this. On Monday morning, we will report to the ground, and we may do a sponsor's appearance before lunch, as we're not allowed to do them during the two days before a match. Next, we will have to do head shots for Sky's TV coverage, before we go on to a signing session where we sign shirts for the PCA partners. After all that, we get a chance to have a training session in the afternoon. In the evening, especially before a Lord's Test, there will be a sponsors' dinner.

On Tuesday, we will have a team meeting to go through the opposition before we go out and have another training session. Andy Flower believes it is important to discuss the opposition first, so we can be thinking about what we're doing in training in the light of what has just been discussed. After lunch, there will be another team meeting, before we do more training in the afternoon. On Wednesday, we'll have some light training relatively early on, so that we have a chance to get away and chill in the afternoon, to ensure we are refreshed and relaxed ahead of the game on the following day. Many players spend that time with their partner or they might go shopping, but mostly it's a time to get our feet up.

Pre-match training with Tim Bresnan at Headingley during the summer of 2012.

When you look at it that way, each Test match can take up to eight days, which is why back-to-back Tests can be so draining for players, as it leaves us almost without a break in between games.

SETTING AN EXAMPLE

While I recognise the importance of behaving well off the pitch, and understand that I have to tread carefully in what I do or say, at the end of the day I am a cricketer. So if there is one place where I really need to set an example to others, it is surely on the cricket field. But this was a lesson, I have to confess, that took some time to learn.

You might recall that when I first came into the England side, I had quite long hair and, being a relatively fresh-faced 20-year-old, some people thought of me as being perhaps a little bit soft. The fact that I seemed to appeal to some young girls only added to the impression that I was some sort of 'boy band' cricketer. Because of this, both our opponents and some in the crowd believed I might buckle under pressure. I would hope that that impression has changed now that they've had a chance to see me in action for a while. In my early days, I had to get used to hearing the Aussies sing 'Dude Looks Like A Lady' at me. But all of this was to mistake appearances for personality; I'm actually quite a hard character, really.

What I had to recognise was that if I was getting that sort of attention, there came a responsibility, too. In my long-haired days, I often used to let my emotions get the better of me, but I think I've matured a lot since then. I use my emotions to help me focus on the task ahead, and so I would say that I set a better example than I used to.

In my early days playing for England, I had quite long hair, and some took this as a sign that I wasn't mentally tough enough.

When I'm on the field, I know my behaviour can have more of an impact on how others behave than I'd expect. The same is true of anyone who wears an England cricket shirt. It is normal to react if something goes wrong in the field, whether it is a dropped catch or a misfield. At any level of the game, a bowler would be disappointed and have to contain his anger. After all, anyone who is playing a game of cricket wants to do well and win.

What is different when playing for England is not so much that there are the hopes of a nation riding on us winning, but the fact that the close-ups from the TV cameras will maximise any sense of frustration or bad behaviour. And as a bowler, I'm particularly vulnerable to this. If someone misfields, both the fielder and the bowler are usually cross about it, but the camera will be fixed on the bowler, not the fielder. The bowler is always the one on show. Indeed, if a batsman gets out, they have the chance to get back into the changing room to vent their frustration, so again the camera doesn't show it. So bowlers have come to be seen as the stroppiest characters in the side, which may be a little harsh. Though I imagine there's a few in the England changing room who might just agree with that statement!

The older I'm getting, the more aware I am of how I behave on the pitch. I am fully committed, and I want that to show (no one likes to see a professional sportsman who doesn't seem to care, and I would hope that no one would ever have cause to think that of me), but it mustn't spill over into bad behaviour. It's a very delicate balancing act: to show the complete commitment that I am giving while not overstepping the mark. I believe it's important that I show people how to play the game in the right spirit, and I've come to realise the effect I can have on kids with the way I behave. I want to show them, as much as I can, the right way to grow up. If I can keep my cool in a pressurised situation in an Ashes Test match, then there's no reason why a young cricketer playing a colts game can't do the same. We all know how much youngsters will copy what they see on

As a bowler, the camera will more often be focused on me than the fielder, which means I have to be careful in how I show my emotions.

television – look at the goal celebrations they come up with that mimic what they've seen Premier League footballers do – and that's why it is so important. I can't claim I always get it right, but I do try.

Of all the issues relating to behaviour on the pitch, arguably the most important thing we as England players have to be seen to do is to respect the umpires' decisions. This is vital, because we don't want kids feeling that it is OK to pressurise umpires and to dispute decisions. Their verdicts must always be respected.

Although some have argued that the Decision Review System (DRS) has undermined the umpire, because his decision is no longer final, I believe it has helped the way we behave. Now, with DRS, if an umpire gives a decision we are sure is wrong, we can go and have another look on replay via the third umpire. There is no big protest, where players gang up round the umpire, and no lingering resentment, but instead the captain, bowler and wicket-keeper get together for a quick discussion and the captain decides if we will call for a review.

The process all looks very civilised and calm, and there is no doubt that it has helped reduce some of the dissent you might have got in an earlier era. When I watch football, I don't understand how players are allowed to get away with some of their behaviour. If the referee makes a bad decision, they're right in his face swearing at him. If someone did that to me in the street, I might feel tempted to punch him, so why do they think it's all right to do it in front of thousands, or millions? By contrast, rugby sets a marvellous example, because if anyone says a word to the referee, they are penalised. That's how it should be in all sports.

HEROES

I must admit that I've never been a great one for having sporting heroes; when I was a boy, I didn't plaster my walls with posters of particular stars. That said, what I look for in someone I admire is the way they play their sport, rather than necessarily focusing on what they have done and achieved in their careers.

As a Nottingham lad, it won't surprise you to hear that Stuart Pearce was someone who stood out to me for the commitment that he showed. To me, he typified everything about the passion of playing for England and for Nottingham Forest. I remember his reaction in Euro 96 when he scored that penalty in the shoot-out – who could ever forget it? He had had a huge disappointment, when he had failed to score in the shoot-out against Germany in Italia 90, but he was brave enough to fight back and step up to take another one when the occasion arose. One of my biggest regrets, however, was that I didn't get the chance to see much of him playing for Forest.

Martin Johnson was another sporting hero of mine. What I admired about him was that he was a character who, so to speak, always threw the first punch – he would lead the way. I remember him running out at the head of the Lions

Sadly, I wasn't even born when Nottingham Forest were European champions.

team carrying a toy lion under his arm and I just thought: 'Wow! What a bloke to do that.' I could tell that he was someone who his team-mates completely respected, and who, in turn, would always back up his team-mates. If someone had a go at one of them, he'd have a go back on their behalf.

What both Pearce and Johnson showed in abundance was their passion for the cause. The same would be true of one of my cricket heroes, Glenn McGrath. He may have looked cross and grumpy for some of the time, but I could tell just how much it meant to him that Australia should succeed. Furthermore, as a fast bowler, he epitomised so many of the qualities that are needed to be a success. I remember just how relentless he was at Lord's in the 2005 Ashes series, when he destroyed England after we had bowled out the Aussies quickly on the first day. He always seemed to bowl well at the ground, perhaps because he had a spell playing for Middlesex. But also, he was one of the few overseas bowlers who understood how to use the slope at Lord's, which can so often throw people out of their rhythm.

Although they are not heroes of mine, I have recently started a hobby whereby I have begun to collect the number eight shirts worn by various famous players – it's the shirt number I wear for England and I've been trying to get hold of them from as many people as I can from across a range of sports. I don't have a special display of the shirts, I simply hang them up on a rail at home so that people can flick through them and see who they discover there.

CROWD SCENE

I've always believed that the mental side of the game should be the same whether I'm playing in front of five devoted followers at Egerton Park or with a crowd of 90,000 at the MCG. However many people are watching, I want to

Glenn McGrath in action at Lord's during the 2005 Ashes series – he was an inspiration to me.

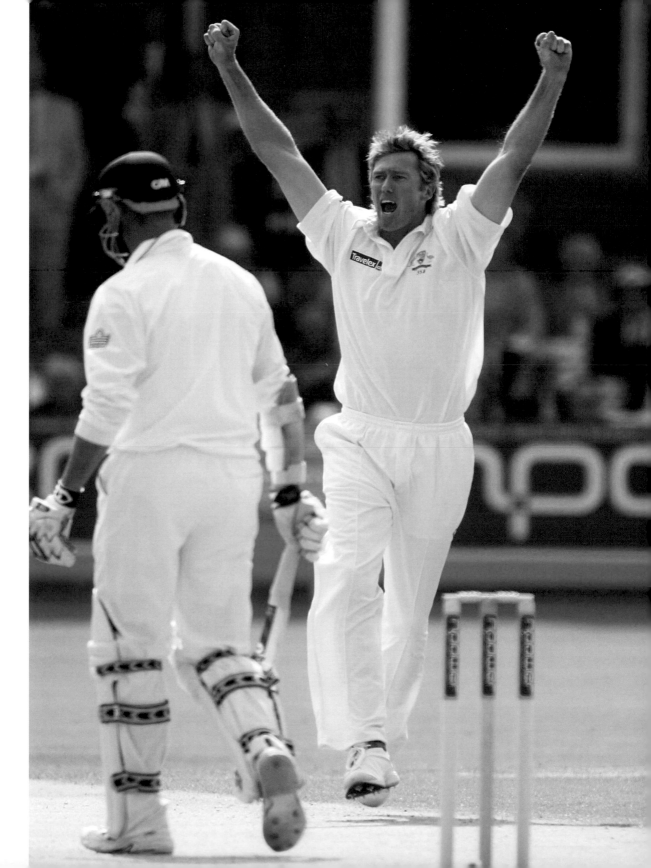

get inside my bubble and focus on the task in front of me: after all, however big the crowd, I still have to bowl the same ball.

Yet, however much that is the aim, it is fair to say that the crowd can have an influence on events, and on the way one is feeling. I've already mentioned how, before I ran in for my hat-trick ball, I could feel the ground bouncing, but I had to shut that out and concentrate simply on bowling my delivery. Whereas when I was facing a hat-trick ball in Australia, I will admit the crowd did distract me to a degree.

In a big crowd, usually all that we can hear is a general roar of noise, but occasionally something else breaks through. I remember in 2007-08 in

The atmosphere in the Brisbane Ashes Test was one of the best I can remember in my career – it almost seemed as if the only Aussies there were on the pitch.

Sri Lanka, there were one or two supporters who were giving us a bit of stick, and it was a really eerie feeling, as usually our fans are incredibly positive and supportive. That sort of criticism – there was a huge banner saying: 'We've paid all this money to come and watch this rubbish' – can really throw you, because cricket isn't like football, where players often get abuse from their own fans. I must admit that being made to feel guilty in that way didn't actually help. Believe me, we are the first ones to know when things are not going right. Being told that watching us was a waste of money certainly made me feel even worse.

The fact that I can remember that particular instance shows just how rare it was. In fact, I would suggest that the England cricket side are the luckiest sporting team in the world with the fans we've got. I'll never forget up at Brisbane in the first Test of the 2010-11 Ashes series, where we made 517 for one in our second innings, what happened when we came out to bowl the last few overs at the end of the final day. The Gabba is a stadium that holds well over 40,000 people, yet when we walked onto the field there was just one stand packed with Englishmen and there didn't seem to be an Aussie in sight. That was a truly special moment and illustrated yet again what great supporters we have. It gave us a huge lift to be so far away from home and yet it seemed as though we were in England.

Sometimes, even the Barmy Army faces an uphill struggle to make themselves heard. In India, the level of attention we get there is unlike anything we come across anywhere else. The fans go mental; we'll have thousands outside our hotel shouting and screaming. It makes it an exciting place to go, but we need to have strong nerves to cope. I remember one particular one-day game we played in India. There were about 55,000 in the crowd that day and we couldn't hear the fitness trainer talking when we were warming up, so deafening was the noise they made – and that was before the game had even started, which merely served to crank up the volume to 11.

If the Barmy Army were drowned out on that occasion, it doesn't happen too often. They probably don't realise the effect they can have on the team when they do their chants, but they really do get the boys going. They bring a lot of energy to us. They come to watch and enjoy the game they love, but they're also there to spur on the players to win the game. The players all like it when they hear the Barmy Army singing for them. The chant they have for me is: 'He's big, he's bad/He's better than his dad/Stuart Broad, Stuart Broad.' It always brings a smile to my face when I hear them singing it.

After I'd been on a few tours, I began to get used to seeing the same guys and girls on the tours, so I got to know some of them. There's one bloke known as Deco (he's a decorator) who is at every Test and he shouts 'Good morning' before every game, so we just give him a wave. We can also go and celebrate with the England fans after we've won, which is unlike anything that would

Signing an autograph for a young England fan – we have the best supporters in the world.

ever happen in football, for example. I think the footballers miss out by not having those same experiences we have.

The celebration that sticks in my mind was in Napier in 2008, where we'd come back from 1-0 down to win the series 2-1 and we ended up in this waterside beach bar and everyone was singing Barmy Army songs. Paul Collingwood

When we are on tour we try not to forget or take for granted what our supporters have to sacrifice to follow us and cheer us on.

was on the bar doing the noises for 'The Lion Sleeps Tonight'. It was one of those great nights – there's no way we could ever do something like that in England, because of the intrusion we'd get. But there, everyone could let their hair down and enjoy themselves – it was great.

For me, the nearest equivalent I have is at the Larwood and Voce pub at Trent Bridge. This is a place we can nip into after a game and have a drink and relax. Because I'm so often away from home, I rarely seem to have much to eat in the house, so it's great to have such a convenient place to come to – especially as the food there is excellent.

But when we are on tour we try not to forget or take for granted what our supporters have to sacrifice to follow us and cheer us on. Sadly, sometimes the host nations try to take advantage of the support we have – for our recent tour to Sri Lanka, the prices they were asking England's fans to pay, compared with every other team, were apparently much higher, so some of them ended up watching the game in Galle from the fort instead. I hope that that won't be repeated in the future, because there's no doubt that having a big crowd in to watch a match makes for a much better atmosphere. It is really unusual for us to have to play in front of sparse crowds, as was the case when we took on Pakistan in the UAE in the previous tour during the winter of 2011-12.

Each of those tours taught us new things, whether it was performing in front of small crowds, dealing with extreme temperatures or working out how to deal with a new type of spin threat. Learning from our experiences, and reviewing what we did right and what we did wrong, has been an important part of England's success. The review process should be a key aspect of any team's development, and that's what we will look at in the next chapter.

A good team will learn lessons from any game, even where everything seems to have gone according to plan.

Chapter 11

REVIEWING

In the England team, we see the review process as just as important as the planning.

So far in this book, we have looked at a whole range of tasks a player or a team needs to undertake if they are to achieve their potential. These include practice, training, planning, tactics and so on. But none of that will be enough if, at the end of the day, little thought is given to whether or not all of that effort has been successful. Reviewing what a team or a player has done during a match is vital. A good team will learn lessons from any game, even the ones where everything seems to have gone according to plan. In the England team, we see the review process as just as important as the planning. And it begins as soon as possible after we come off the field.

DON'T LOOK BACK IN ANGER

Good sports teams tend to keep negative language to a minimum, so when one of England's batsmen comes back into the changing room after getting out, he won't say how unplayable it is out in the middle, piling on descriptions of the agonies that await the rest of the batting order. Equally, if conditions are tough, no one wants to be lulled into a false sense of security. So there has to be a great deal of frank assessment from the dismissed batsman; if it is difficult, he has to tell the rest of us waiting to go in that it is really challenging

In the England team, the dismissed batsman tries to give honest feedback on what the rest of the side can do to counter the threat.

out there. But it's what he says next that is crucial. The batsman will start suggesting possible solutions to the problems he has faced, in the hope that those coming in after him can be not only better prepared, but can also start working out how they plan to combat the situation when the time comes. It's essential teamwork, even after the pain of being dismissed.

Of course, I wouldn't ask an incoming batsman for his thoughts the moment he came back to the changing room. When someone has just got out for their country, he's obviously disappointed and so there may be some swearing and banging, but people soon recover from that. Once that time has passed, I feel I can then ask: 'Is it a dangerous shot to try driving out of the rough?' Or whatever it is that I might need to know. To which he might reply that I'd be better off trying to work the ball through the on side. No one should ever be scared to ask a question of a batsman who's been out. Even with someone like Jonathan Trott, who takes a little longer than most to get over being out, it's still OK to ask. That said, I must admit it can be handy that there are three or four rooms in the home changing room when we play at Trent Bridge, so that one or two people can move away from the rest of us for some time alone – not mentioning any names. But the key thing is this: at any level of cricket, this sort of dialogue must be able to take place for the sake of the team, or else those lower down the order are going in to bat without all the information they need.

In any player's career, he's always likely to get out to some great balls, especially when he's up against the very best bowlers or batting on a difficult track. The easy thing to do is to say: 'That was too good for me.' But in fact, it's rare to receive a ball that is so good you couldn't have done anything about it. It's much better to face up to the truth: most dismissals are down to batsman error. The mistake will often have been caused by bowlers creating pressure, which forces a batter either into playing a rash shot or simply to lose concentration. As a batsman, if I sense the pressure mounting on me, I focus on where my scoring areas are and try to stick to my gameplan. If I can be relaxed about that, then I can afford to bide my time.

Even as we walk off the pitch, we know we will soon be conducting our review into what happened.

> **After we come off the pitch, the captain and the coach will go through the day and assess how we have performed.**

People sometimes ask me how badly some people take it when they're out. I have to say that the old-style response of throwing your bat when you've got out has pretty much died out. That said, I do remember, in my early days at Leicestershire, one guy who when he came back in would take off his kit and then go and whack the telly with his pad, saying: 'That wasn't out!' We just looked at him as if to say 'pull yourself together!' I can't say I've seen much of that sort of behaviour since then – we tend to be more philosophical now.

While that sort of feedback is ongoing during a match, we will also review each day's play during a Test. After we come off the pitch, the captain and the coach will go through the day and assess how we have performed. There will be food on the ground, for those who want to stay there and perhaps talk things through in greater detail, but most people will go back to the hotel or go out with their friends or family. The tone during this review at the end of the day is usually quite light, as everyone is tired. After that, the bowlers will sit in a corner with bowling coach David Saker and we'll assess what we've got right and wrong: should we change our lines? What about moving a slip a bit wider? The focus is on small details, rather than on the big picture.

The reviews we have in the morning before we start again are a bit more intense. It makes sense to do the serious reviews then, when we've had a chance to get the emotion out of it, which isn't always possible at the end of the day. In these sessions, we will look at how we can do better, and how can we keep driving forward. It is important that we put any outstanding issues to bed from the previous day or the previous Test, and move forward. We try not to have any unresolved problems lingering for any longer than necessary.

Because we're a bunch of competitive guys, those review sessions can be very honest. Andy Flower will lead them, and he will always challenge us, asking us if we did this or that well enough. He'll put us on the spot. Then, in front of 15 mates, one of us may have to admit that he let the side down. It's such an important aspect of being a sportsman to be able to do those things and admit responsibility for our errors. We have got very good at that in the England side, and I can definitely say that it helps to build trust between us.

While the level of intensity may be different in a Test side, this review process is something that I believe is a really vital way that any cricketer can develop his game. Of course, the way we do it is highly analytical and the conversations are led by people who know the game inside out, but something similar can happen after just about any cricket match. And the place it usually happens in club cricket is in the bar.

The important thing for any young cricketer to remember – and this may seem quite old school – is that it is possible to do a lot of learning in the bar. It is something that the Aussies have perhaps grasped better than we do, and I'm convinced it helps. It's one of the easiest ways to learn, too: sit there with a drink and chat to the guys about what has just happened.

In the England set-up, the review process is always ongoing.

I remember doing a lot of that in my first year in the county game, but sadly it is now quite hard for players to find the time to do this, often because they are having to travel on to the next game immediately afterwards, so there is no time to reflect.

In the England side, we're very strict on trying to recreate that old-style approach now. There might not necessarily be any alcohol involved, but if someone gets a hundred or a five-fer during the day, we all sit in the changing room together and have a chat, because that's where we have a chance to find out how a batsman was picking a spinner, or how a bowler was able to get on top of a particular batsman. We learn so much from that half-hour's chat – I'd advise any sports team to do it, because it is amazing what can be picked up during that time. Talking leads into trial and error: if I hear that someone has done something that has worked, I might then try that the next time I practise. It can be as simple as slightly moving my thumb position on the ball – if I can gain one new idea from the post-match conversation, then it has to be time well spent.

The England side also uses plenty of video analysis to maximise our ability to review what we've done. Fortunately, from my point of view, we have kept such analysis in the family. Quite literally, for it is my sister Gemma who is in charge of the video analysis for England.

Gemma doesn't do any coaching or anything like that, so there's no sense of her telling her brother what to do on the cricket field. The way we use her skills is to ask her to provide the relevant clips we need, so that we can discuss them with the coaches. It's probably just as well for family harmony that that is how it works!

Different people use video in different ways and to a greater or lesser extent. Personally, I'm not a great believer in watching myself in action for technical analysis. I tend not to watch what I've done wrong, but use video to look at what I've done right.

My sister Gemma is in charge of the video analysis for the England team.

Fortunately, however, not everyone works in the same way, as I was lucky enough to find out very early on in my career.

WHAT ARE THE REVIEWS LIKE?

Soon after I came into the county game, the ECB took some footage of me bowling. What they saw made them decide to make me one of their poster boys – to show how not to do it! It was former England bowling coach Troy Cooley who first told me that I was cashing cheques my body couldn't deliver. Strange as it may seem, when I was 17 and 18, I couldn't raise my right arm straight so that it could touch my ear in my bowling action, and I had to compensate for this fact in my delivery.

Cooley explained that what I was doing could have caused a stress fracture quite easily, but I was lucky that it was spotted then, because I'd only just started to bowl quickly after I'd shot up in height. Had I bowled much longer while still having that problem, the chances are I would have picked up quite a serious injury. The reason I couldn't touch my ear was something to do with my lats, and so they would hang me upside down to help sort out the problem – it was like some sort of Chinese torture. I suppose it was because I'd grown so fast at that time that my lats hadn't caught up with the changes in my body.

There's no doubt I was very lucky to have the problem spotted so early and rectified quickly. After my first year in first-class cricket, they made sure I didn't bowl at all during the winter, but instead we spent the time concentrating on how to get things right with my action and my body so that I was minimising the strain. It was a winter spent getting me ready to bowl for the rest of my career. Even 15 years ago, they would probably have just left me to go on as I was until my body gave way. It was another reason why I have been so lucky in the timing of my career.

Of course, not all review sessions have such long-lasting significance, but some others do stand out in the memory. I remember one important

After a winter spent hanging upside down, I worked on my bowling action to make sure I wasn't putting my body under undue stress.

meeting when we went to Henley and we saw an ex-SAS officer called Floyd Woodrow. He was one of the youngest ever to be selected for the SAS and he told us about some of the battles he'd been involved in (he won a DCM while serving in Afghanistan). But what he talked about was not his own heroics, or those who were fighting with him, but

something that might seem mundane by comparison. He explained how they planned for action, and how they reviewed, analysed and evaluated everything about every operation they undertook.

It made us realise the importance of this process if any task was to be carried out successfully – in our case, of course, lives were not at stake, just the outcome of a cricket match, but the principle is the same. From that day, we've always been very strict on analysing what's happened, recognising our mistakes as well as what we've done right, so that we can then move forward.

We don't just review how the team performed, we each also have a personal review, where we look at what we did in a game: how we got out, how we took wickets, and so on. We're very lucky with the analysts we have: the bowlers each get a print-out of our Hawkeye stats – the percentages of lengths we hit, the percentage of times we're going to hit the stumps, number of times the batsmen played and missed. The information we can get is seemingly limitless, so it is quite possible to get bogged down with it all.

Because of this, I believe it is important not to see the statistics as the be-all and end-all of how I assess my performance. If the bowling coach suggests I've been bowling too short, the figures can provide concrete evidence for his comments. But I also know that if I aim to hit the top of off stump, the chances are that I will do well. In short, the technology might have changed, but the logic of cricket is still the same. The statistics merely back up the old logic of what makes a good ball or a bad one. Sometimes I find that the statistics can just reinforce my good feelings at the end of a day: I think I bowled well, and the stats show that I did too. But, essentially, I think any bowler worth his salt should know that without having to check it all up on the computer.

But there are certainly ways that computers can help us, as long as we use them sensibly. For example, the bowling coach will look at the opposition batsman's scoring areas to see how his wagon wheel looks. Sometimes this merely reflects where we have bowled at him, but it can also illustrate where he is strong and where he likes to hit the ball, so we will try to do something about it to stop him scoring.

Yet again, however, a bowler shouldn't have to wait until the end of the day to pick this up: it's part and parcel of being a cricketer to notice these things while bowling at someone and to do something about it. In the England side, the bowlers will talk about it among themselves during play. If a batsman's scoring a large proportion of his runs on the leg side, we might decide to drag him a bit wider to stop his main scoring strokes and hope that this either frustrates him or forces him to play across the line.

Who needs computer analysis to see that things aren't going according to plan here against South Africa this summer.

ENGLAND MATERIAL

I've occasionally been asked what it was that made the England selectors pick me out so soon after I had made my debut on the county scene. It's a question that makes me review myself, to some degree. What I can definitely say is that, again, I was very lucky in the timing of my career. In years gone by, players often had to serve their dues on the county circuit for much longer than I had to. And the same is true of others in the England squad.

Jimmy Anderson and I were both given early opportunities in the England set-up. We got our chances after just one and a half seasons in county cricket, and to a certain degree have learned our trade in international cricket. Jimmy has evolved hugely as a player; his action now is superb, though he says he has reverted to something similar to his original action.

We both started off as quite scrawny lads with nothing on us, and we hoped that the England set-up could develop what natural talent we had. Duncan Fletcher, my first England coach, always talked about wanting to build his side around 90 mph bowlers. He was a great believer that speed was essential if a bowler was to have a chance in international cricket. So the fact that I had pace got me noticed.

Having made my debut for England in limited-overs cricket in 2006, I then spent the next two winters with the Academy, learning my trade. I think Jimmy also had a spell with them, too. I have little doubt that this experience helped us develop as players, and probably as people, too. Once we had been identified as England contenders, we were lucky that they stuck by us and they backed us. This wasn't something that always happened within the England set-up ten or 20 years ago. Even though the England coaches have changed a few times since I've been around – Fletcher was succeeded by Peter Moores, who then gave way to Andy Flower – there has been plenty of consistency in the sides that have been selected.

Some of this stability has come from whichever coach has been in place, but we have also had more consistency from the England selectors, who watch a lot of cricket and talk to the county coaches in great detail to find out what is happening there. I was fortunate in Leicestershire that I was with Tim Boon, who had been in the England set-up, while Jimmy was with Lancashire's Mike Watkinson, who had also been involved with England. Their opinions on our potential were valued, and they could speak from experience about what was required to play at the very top. If Fletcher or the selectors had asked them

Working with Peter Moores, one of the England coaches during my time in the side.

if we'd got what it takes to make it, and they had backed us, then their views would have carried weight.

How it works is that the selectors will explain to the coach what a certain player offers, and the coach will then decide if that fits in with what the side needs. Both Jimmy and I did quite well in our first full season of county cricket: I took 48 wickets in 2006, for example, which was a pretty strong start. It's not as though we were picked from nowhere; we'd got some good players out and we'd put our names out there as guys with potential.

The selectors have often been criticised over the years, but I think they deserve credit for identifying people and sticking with them. Look at Alastair Cook, who had such a tough time of it in the summer of 2010. There was a great deal of media pressure to say he shouldn't go to Australia for the Ashes, but the selectors stuck by him, and he repaid their faith. I am sure they understood that not only does he have terrific ability, but his character is strong. Again, it's not clear that the policy would have been the same in earlier times.

I think we all have to trust that the selectors and coaches know what they're looking for, and judge them on their results. As for what that might be, well, I remember my dad saying to me when I was 14 that cricket is 90 per cent mental and 10 per cent technical. At the time, I was surprised at that, but as I've grown older and had to face up to the challenges of top-level cricket, I have recognised that it is character that gets a player through and takes them where they want to go.

A good example of how the selectors searched for character and temperament would be Michael Vaughan and Marcus Trescothick. Given his recent prolific form in the county game, it might surprise some people to know that before Tres went on tour with England A during the winter of 1999-00, he averaged just under 30 with the bat after seven seasons in the first-class game. Vaughan was another who didn't do anything particularly special in the county game before his call-up. But put them in the Test arena and their average was much higher. For example, Vaughan averaged under 37 in first-class cricket but over 41 in Tests. Equally, there was a time in 2002 or

2003 when Trescothick's first-class average was 34 and his Test average was over 40. Had Trescothick not ended his Test career, his numbers now would be astonishing. But those two are perfect examples of picking someone for England on character and then them proving they have what it takes.

Vaughan was someone who, if you put him up against someone swinging the ball at 75 mph, could hardly lay a bat on it, but have him up against the real quicks in the pressure of a Test match and he was a world-beater. Of the current generation, Cooky's probably the one who is the most similar to those two – the harder the challenge the better he seems to play. Yet when Saurav Ganguly bowled at him, he seemed to cause him more problems than some of India's frontline bowlers.

If I had to summarise what characteristics the selectors are looking for when they make their recommendations, I would say they look for those who perform in tough scenarios: have they won games for their county? Have they scored runs or taken wickets when they are most needed by their side? Have they taken five-fer on a flat wicket? I think character is revealed by when someone performs as much as by how they perform. Andrew Strauss talks about this when he says he wants bowlers who never suffer from flatwicketitis – those bowlers who always want to have the ball in their hands and still have a go. I would argue that those conditions not only reveal one's character, but they are the times when one learns the most.

REVIEWING THE FUTURE

I'll know I've made it as a cricketer when I stop getting called Chris. My dad's never been pushy, but there's no doubt he has helped me in my career. Because he's been involved in the game at the top level, he knows what it's like and we

Michael Vaughan was one of those players who thrived on the intensity of international cricket.

can talk about issues that other fathers wouldn't perhaps be able to understand as well as he can, for that reason. Furthermore, he's still involved in the game as a match referee, so he knows what's happening in other countries we are due to visit and what the pitches are like there. So, when we were heading off to Sri Lanka earlier in the year, he could give me advice about what to expect.

I suppose when it comes to people making comparisons between us, my biggest blessing is that I'm a bowling all-rounder, while he was an opening batsman, so although we're in the same sport, we're not directly comparable in what we do. If I had been an opening batsman, people would always have

Action from the game in Dubai in January 2012 – these days touring sides rarely have much time to adapt to unfamiliar conditions.

been telling me that he played this shot better, or he'd got more runs than I had by that stage. Instead, I get comments on how the occasional shot I play looks like one of his, despite the fact that I'm a bowler – and that's brilliant for me. I do think some of my shots look like his – obviously not to the same level of success as him. I hope one day I can catch up with him as far as the number of Test centuries we've both scored.

But personal considerations really aren't important to me. It is the team that is important. We went into the summer of 2012 as the top-ranked Test nation in the world. A 2-0 win over the West Indies kept us there, before we faced up to South Africa in the latter part of the season. Following on from big series wins against Australia and India, this was another big one for us: if South Africa won the series they would overhaul us at the top of the rankings.

But that sort of pressure is how we like it: world cricket is extremely competitive at the moment, especially as it is proving hard for teams to win away from home. Perhaps that's because it takes a while for players to get used to strange conditions, but with the schedule as it is now, there aren't the same sort of long tours that would last for months on end and allow visiting sides to acclimatise fully.

Our aim is not just to be number one but to become the standout team in world cricket, as the West Indies were for so long, and then Australia. We want to create an enduring legacy as being one of the great teams in history. But at the moment, between us, Australia, India and South Africa anyone can beat anyone on their day. We want to change that; we want the rest to fear us.

The way we will do that is by finally proving ourselves in the subcontinent. We're a very good team in England: our batsmen score lots of runs in swinging conditions and our bowlers take lots of wickets. However, our technique was shown up a little bit in subcontinental conditions against Pakistan and Sri Lanka, and that is something we are looking to work on. Even the Australian side of the 1990s struggled in India. It's not just the pitch conditions that are so different: Sri Lanka was the hardest physical test of my career. During the

I will keep on working at my game so that I can continue to fulfil my dreams, playing for England.

warm-up game in Colombo, it was 46°C, but it got to 51°C in the middle.

In those conditions, it was possible to bowl three, maybe four, overs in a spell, and after that I was gone. I think we coped with it quite well, all things considered. When keeping, Matt Prior lost 4kg in weight by tea, to give some idea of how intense the heat was. But we're fortunate that we can have drinks breaks and wear ice vests; I can't imagine how they coped in the old days when they didn't have scheduled drinks breaks.

We also focused on making sure the nutrition we took on at lunch and tea was as good as possible, we stayed out of the sun whenever we could, and we all wore sun hats. But I think we passed the physical tests with flying colours. Trotty was able to bat long and score a hundred. That's real mental strength, and it is vital to have that if we're going to win out there.

When we were talking to the guys from the Barmy Army after the game, they were saying they didn't know how we managed to run around there, as they were flagging just sitting watching us. But something about playing for England and for the team got us through it, even when our concentration was getting zapped by the heat.

If we have learned anything from our experiences in early 2012, it was that we have gained confidence that we can take wickets in those conditions. If we can find our way to scoring big runs out there too, we'll be hard to stop. We will have our chance this winter in the twenty20 World Cup in Sri Lanka and in the Test series against India, and I hope we can return with victories in both. And after that, we have back-to-back Ashes series to look forward to. And so it goes on, one challenge follows another – I wouldn't have it any other way. That's why I will keep on working at my game, and keep on trying to find new ways I can improve at what I do, so that I can continue to fulfil my dreams, playing for England. I hope that what I have written in here will help and inspire you to fulfil your dreams, too, and to play the best cricket that you can. Give it a try and see where it takes you.

ACKNOWLEDGEMENTS

There are many people I have to thank for their help in putting this book together. First, my thanks go to Tim Boon for all his work drawing up the training exercises featured in these pages. My thanks also go to Nottinghamshire CCC and the staff at Trent Bridge for allowing me to shoot many of the pictures in the book at various locations in the ground.

Speaking of the photography, apart from the pictures from my childhood, all the images in here were taken by Philip Brown, who did a superb job, risking life and lens to get close to the action in the indoor nets.

I would also like to thank Neil Fairbrother and Tracy Gaffey at my management company, International Sports Management, for their help and support.

At the publishers, Simon & Schuster, my thanks go to Rhea Halford, Matt Johnson, Kyle McEnery, Kerr MacRae, Ian Marshall and the rest of the team there for their work in putting the book together with me. Jacqui Caulton did a wonderful job on designing the pages.

Finally, I would like to thank Mum, Dad, Gemma and Nick for all their help, not just with the writing of this book, but with so much else.